About the au

Tim Hartley thinks his next best experience is around the corner, so he just keeps on travelling. He was a journalist with the BBC and a civil servant. He has also worked as a consultant in Europe, Central Asia and Africa. Hartley has an unhealthy interest in post-communist regimes and football. He has written about his obsession for the BBC's *From Our Own Correspondent* programme and for a number of newspapers and magazines. Hartley lives in Cardiff with his son Chester, who shares his interests, and his wife Helen, who humours them both. His mother-in-law in Port Talbot once said to him, "How many trips of a lifetime can you have, boy?"

KICKING OFF IN NORTH KOREA

Football and Friendship in Foreign Lands

To Chester

'Mae'r daith ond megis dechrau'

KICKING OFF IN NORTH KOREA

Football and Friendship in Foreign Lands

TIM HARTLEY

First impression: 2016

© Copyright Tim Hartley and Y Lolfa Cyf., 2016

The contents of this book are subject to copyright, and may
not be reproduced by any means, mechanical or electronic,
without the prior, written consent of the publishers.

The publishers wish to acknowledge the support of
Cyngor Llyfrau Cymru

Cover design: Paz Martínez Capuz

ISBN: 978 1 78461 244 3

Published and printed in Wales
on paper from well-maintained forests by
Y Lolfa Cyf., Talybont, Ceredigion SY24 5HE
website www.ylolfa.com
e-mail ylolfa@ylolfa.com
tel 01970 832 304
fax 832 782

Contents

Preface

THE MARKET PLACE in Ramallah is a riot of colour and smells. They assault your senses as you battle through the frantic crowd. Pomegranates and oranges tumble onto the street, outsized grapefruit and baby aubergines like shiny plastic toy food, green leaves of all shades and shapes, bundles of fresh mint, an old woman piling maple shaped leaves bigger than her hand into neat piles on top of a tea chest at the side of the road. The shouts and pitching of the stall holders. Some sing-song, another hits you sharp with a yelp. I instinctively look round. No-one else is listening, just me, but it doesn't stop the traders. Juicers oozing reds and purples, limes and carrots and lemons dribbling into plastic cups and onto the dusty pavement. Cardamom and thyme, rosemary, coriander and cumin mix and blend and then one herb reasserts its own zing. There! Smack in the face. Fresh unleavened bread like an outsized pizza base stretched on a strange metal mushroom, tossed into a rotobaker to pop out lovely and brown, ready to be torn into finger-sized dippers for the hummus, tomato and onion salad. "Mmm," says my son Chester, "that's cleared my sinuses."

Ramallah, for now the capital of the Palestinian Territories, once home to Yasser Arafat, the revolutionary turned statesman who became president. His mausoleum is here, not far from the central market, in the Mukataa, his proto government's first proper home. Flanked by two soldiers the tomb is of beige Jerusalem stone and is surrounded on three sides by water. A piece of rail track is entombed underneath Arafat's grave. The water and track symbolise the temporary nature of the grave. The Palestinians will rebury their leader one day in Jerusalem, their hoped-for permanent capital.

Frankly there's not a lot in Ramallah. It's a bit of a dump really. The centre is an unplanned knot of ramshackle off-white buildings thrown up along narrow streets where the traffic toots and the vendors dodge one another day and night. It's dusty and messy. Just another untidy Arab town. Ramallah is not on most people's tourist agenda. It is unremarkable, yes, boring maybe, but captivating too because it buzzes with life.

A half-hour's drive from here the pilgrims were flocking to Jerusalem to celebrate Easter. The alleys of the Old Town were packed as Christians carrying wooden crosses, some in hand, others so heavy they needed three people to drag them over the cobbles, sang and cried their way up the Via Dolorosa to the Church of the Holy Sepulchre, the site of His crucifixion and burial. They sang in English, then came the turn of the Russians, was that Armenian? And tantalisingly, in Arabic. That's why you go to the Holy Land isn't it? To follow in the footsteps of Christ and to breathe the Old Testament in the ruins of Jericho and the Sea of Galilee. Well, yes and no.

Of course you can visit the sacred Christian sights, but get off the tourist drag and you can see the plight of the Palestinians. On your way to that photo op in the Dead Sea you can view the dramatic Ma'ale Adumim Israeli settlement in the West Bank. You can't miss it. It towers above Route One on the road east from Jerusalem, a symbol of Israeli incursion and conquest. These ancient civilisations are laid out here, alongside one another, for anyone to see.

But can you see any of these places, objects and people unmediated? When our world view is shaped, however unwittingly, by our own cultural narrative, by the media, politicians, religion and our own prejudices, how can we truly understand this world? Maybe we can't. Maybe what we see, what we think we see, is all a construct narrated by the forces of geo politics. But I like to think I have tried and at times had some sort of revelation, a little insight into what things are really like. It wasn't always comfortable and at a checkpoint in North Korea, in the back of a stranger's car in Belarus, on an overnight train to Chisinau or in a dodgy favela in Brazil, I asked myself why? My self-doubt never lasted long. Perversely, the more I am pushed, questioned, hassled or simply tired out, the more I like to think I connect even if I will never truly understand. Sympathy, not empathy, perhaps.

My wife Helen says I like grottiness for its own sake, that I always seek the ground-floor view. She's probably right but she knows that travelling like this is when I come alive. She also knows when it's time for me to go. "Itchy feet again, darling?" she says pityingly every couple of months, "Off you go then." Bless her!

This book is not a call to travelling arms and I am not saying that if you have not experienced the 'real thing' then you weren't actually there. There are so many real things. I can tell you about the splendours of the lost pink city that is Petra or the majesty of Chichen Itza. But I would rather talk about the decline of the Sami people and their reindeer herding life, the young men trying to revitalise the Basque language and the reinvention of the Mayans in the Yucatán. These trips, abroad and at home, were made for a variety of reasons – the sheer joy of travelling, 'educational' visits for our son, for football, for family, for my work as a journalist or supporting the football charity Gôl!

Of course you don't have to travel a million miles to be amazed and enthused. Some of my best adventures have been right here in the UK, in a quaint market town in Oxfordshire or a gritty suburb in east London. Like a child in a forest I just have to open my eyes and I am intrigued and fascinated by the ordinary as well as the extraordinary. The street in Ramallah could be my own Cowbridge Road in Cardiff. That too has shops and stalls, people and traffic. But they aren't the same. Are they? Culture may be reflected in what people have left behind, fine objects and grand buildings. To me though it is more about the people themselves, the way they speak, the things they do and the way they live. Is this 'seek and see' thing of mine a passion or an obsession? I don't know but come along with me while I carry on searching until I find some sort of answer, or until my time is up.

Tim Hartley
Cardiff, 2016

"Dad, we hate the Israelis, don't we?"

February 2001

WE FOLLOWED THE coast road north of Beirut and turned up a steep incline. The whole hillside was spattered with higgledy-piggledy white buildings. An unplanned, urban sprawl which stretched forever. The city eventually sank back to the sea behind us, we crossed the mountains and found ourselves in the Beqaa Valley, destination Baalbek, the Phoenician-cum-Hellenistic-cum-Roman architectural masterpiece. I didn't expect the valley to be so wide or the land so fertile. The Middle East, green? If it weren't for the shimmering sun and broad, clear skies we could have been in Scotland.

Our car slowed down as a man in military uniform stepped out of his sentry box at the side of the road. The box was made of wooden slats and the Lebanese flag had been painted on its side. The red and white stripes followed the rough planks from the tiny roof to the ground and the green cedar of Lebanon sat proudly, if a little washed out, between them. It was a little like a toy sentry box. The soldier inside, though, was all too real.

"No problem. No problem," said our driver sensing our unease as the soldier moved towards the car. "Lebanese army. It's OK. Yeah. OK." And so it was. Our papers checked, we headed north. Being so wide, the floor of the Beqaa Valley is remarkably flat and the hills seem far away and hazy.

Just a mile or so down the road we were flagged down again. Another soldier with an assault rifle slung on his back but this time wearing a different coloured uniform. Sitting in the middle of the Mercedes taxi, I squeezed my wife and Chester's hands. The soldier poked his head through the driver's window, saw this strange young family with a tiny blond boy sitting meekly in the back and waved us on. This one, we were told, was from the Syrian Army. Two miles on there was yet another checkpoint. Only this guy was unshaven, wore a leather jacket and had an AK47 riding around his hip. Words were exchanged between the taxi driver and the militia man and we drove away.

"So who was that, then?" I whispered.

"Ah," said our driver almost respectfully, "That – Hezbollah." Hmm – the Party of God. And on we went.

Helen looked at me. Her pursed lips told me what she'd voiced two months earlier. "Half-term in Beirut? Lebanon? You are joking, aren't you?" I'd done my research, I'd told her.

"It'll be an educational tour. Good for the lad. You know, experience new cultures and all that. Nothing to worry about." Though I admit I neglected to tell her that Israeli warplanes had recently flown over Lebanon and bombed a power station, not far from here actually.

The whole week was an education, and not just for the boy. Back in Beirut we played football with a light, plastic, red ball across our ridiculously large bedroom. Ever the conscientious teacher, Helen was doing schoolwork and was not amused when our stray shots hit her. "Goal!" shouted Chester and we sniggered. I think we gestured to each other and tried to get her again. Since 1991 the war in Lebanon was officially 'over' and the city was in a building frenzy. Plush hotels were going up everywhere, though we seemed to be the only guests on the seventeenth floor of our tower block. Chester, who was a bubbly seven year old, was getting bored with the Roman ruins of Baalbek, the pockmarked buildings and my obsession with the Palestinian refugees.

"Dad?" (How can a child turn a single syllable into a four-note plea?) "Dad? Can we go and watch some proper football?"

"I dunno, son." I tried to sound authoritative and knocked a ball straight at his face. "Not the season here, is it?"

At which the little tyke produced a neatly folded copy of the *Daily Star*, 'the Middle East's English-language daily newspaper,' as the paper's banner proudly proclaimed. I had given it a cursory glance in the hotel lobby but thought nothing more. Behind the sterile photos of high-level business meetings and billion dollar oil contracts, at the back of the paper, was Chester's *coup de grâce*. He unfolded the pages slowly as if savouring a birthday present and revealed the sports section. The headline read, 'Lebanon Cup semi-final: Shabab Al-Sahel v Nejmeh, kick-off 5.30 p.m.' How could I refuse?

We took a taxi to a dilapidated sports ground with a single soldier on duty at the heavy metal gates. "No. No football here sir."

Our driver also looked confused as we repeated, "Football, football. Big game." We crossed the city and headed out towards the airport. At last the vast angular floodlights of the international stadium reared up before us. A fitting ground for a cup semi-final we thought. Chester was wriggling in his seat. But this place too was empty with not even an armed guard to help us on our way. Not such a big game then.

Helen was getting restless. "It'll be half-time by the time we get there. Come on, let's go home." But the lad was not to be deterred and after an hour's driving and gesticulation we got our reward.

The Beirut Municipal Stadium is a low-lying concrete oval basin, a massive grey ashtray surrounded by tatty high-rise flats with crumbling balconies set in a dowdy residential neighbourhood. The bowl looked as if it had been picked up by a giant alien and just plonked there. It could feature on one of those posters students hang in their rooms alongside the cartoon of the tennis court on top of a skyscraper, the balls bouncing down to the streets below. By the time we arrived the floodlights were on and the edges of the bowl cut sharp, silhouettes against the flats giving the evening an unreal feel.

We stood among a few hundred supporters all wearing the de rigueur fashion item for Lebanese men, a shiny black leather bomber jacket. They dipped into white paper cones, nibbled on tiny nuts, spitting out the shells as they talked among themselves. The crowd was poor and the football itself was awful. It seems that a semi-final in Beirut is just another night out for the men (there were no women, bar Helen, to be seen) – a chance to chat with the lads. Some of them threw looks in our direction. The white family with a woman and a little blond boy. Then one of them approached us, his hand outstretched with a packet of biscuits for the aliens. We took one each, smiled and said, *"Shokran gazillan,"* as we'd been taught by the taxi driver. Then the young man gestured to Chester. "Come. Speak English," he said and led our little boy down the terrace and around the back of the goal to where he and his mates were standing.

We kept a distant, if watchful, eye on proceedings and saw Chester chatting with his new friends. It was half-time and I needed the toilet. I walked to the back of the stand and stopped in my tracks. A row of some fifteen men were on their knees before the wire fence on the uncovered concourse which looked into the flats beyond. It was that time of day and they were facing Mecca in prayer. Their devotion, as they rocked back and forth, was evident and I felt slightly humbled, as if I was intruding on their collective but private moment.

Chester wound his way back over the crumbling steps of the terrace.

"Alright son?" I asked, not sure what he would be able to tell me of his lone meeting with the Shabab faithful.

There was a slight pause and then he said, almost to himself, "We hate the Israelis don't we, Dad?"

Helen and I looked at each other, for once both lost for words. Our educational tour of the Middle East had just taken on a very different meaning.

The Ambassador, the Queen and the Man United fan

August 2003

TEALIGHT CANDLES IN small jam jars twinkled along the low walls of the deputy ambassador's residence. Under a gentle green canopy in a discreet suburb of Belgrade there was a low, respectful buzz of conversation in the night heat. The British Embassy was keen to build bridges and make friends and one way of doing that was through showing the acceptable face of British football. Officials of the Football Association of Wales in regulation blazers and ties and we, the fans, in our replica tops mixed with local journalists and politicians in anticipation of the Wales versus Serbia European qualifier match.

The country was still raw from the collapse of Yugoslavia as the redrawing of the Balkan map dragged on. It was just four years since the UK and America had bombed what was then still the capital of Yugoslavia, Belgrade, as the 'Allies' tried to get Slobodan Milošević to relax his bloody grip on the disputed province of Kosovo. We'd seen the damage ourselves: a ministry building downtown with a ten-foot hole blown in its front, windowless, its crumbling grey concrete left as a grim reminder of the all-too-recent history. The football match we'd come to watch had been postponed after the Serb prime minister, Zoran Đinđić, was killed by a single sniper's shot in March as he walked into the main government building.

But tonight, friendship through football was the order of the day and with the offer of free beer and those delicious canapés you only ever see at receptions like this, the Wales fans were only too happy to play their part as peacemakers. Our national team was for once doing rather well and hopes were high of qualification for the 2004 finals in Portugal. The Wales supporters had played a charity match that afternoon against a local side. The Ambassador himself had turned up with his children to play. They'd emerged from a bulletproof car and had a minder close at hand. The younger son made a bit of a faux pas by wearing England football socks. Now the Embassy wanted to thank us and at the party we were introduced to the movers and shakers of Serbian football.

Zoran Milosavljevic was a young and thrusting football reporter. He worked for Reuters and had a wicked sense of humour. After a recent poor performance by the local team Zoran had opened his article paraphrasing club officials, "Red Star Belgrade players must stop eating meat pies for breakfast, drinking beer after practice and enjoying wild nights out in the Serbian capital." Zoran had a pudgy face, a shaved head and an earring in his left ear. He looked like he belonged on the terraces rather than in the press box. As a mutual lover of football he was keen to make friends. He took great pride in introducing us to Dragan Stojković, one of Yugoslavia's best players, the former captain of Red Star and the national team – who played eighty-four times for his country. Chester was now nine years old and chuffed to have his picture taken with a real, professional footballer, even one he'd never heard of.

Inside the official British residence under an ageing picture of the Queen short speeches thanking everyone for everything were given drawing polite applause, and then it was time to go. As we sped back to the city centre, Zoran told us about Red Star's season and we discussed Wales' prospects. But most of all he wanted to discuss his team, not Red Star or Partizan, nor any Yugoslav or Serb team. No, Zoran's team was Manchester United. "I really love them. My favourite player is your man

Ryan Giggs. I wish I could show you my flat. It's like a shrine to them. Posters, scarves. I've got the lot." He talked about players, past and present, the great games he had watched on satellite TV or had read about. The Ambassador, I am sure, would have been pleased by the success of this particular element of British cultural outreach.

The Irish bar was as dark inside as the deputy ambassador's garden had been under the autumn night. We sat at a high table facing each other which forced us into an intimacy with a guy we had only just met. Zoran was enthusiastic about everything but he discussed politics only in abstraction. He knew about the wars and had suffered himself as the after-effects hit Belgrade. He wouldn't take sides, at least not in front of us. "It's all wrong. Just crazy," he said, exasperated.

Zoran asked about politics in the UK and was interested in Wales, the Welsh language and the new National Assembly. I enthused about a young democracy and our high hopes for the future thinking it would resonate with his now smaller but still fervent nation.

"We had a fantastic celebration to open the Assembly," I said. "Tom Jones and Shirley Bassey sang. We even had the Queen sitting behind us in Cardiff Bay." Then I thought of a great parallel which he could relate to. "It was the same night Man U played Bayern Munich in the Champions League final. 1999. You must remember it. It was at the Camp Nou in Barcelona." Zoran looked uneasy but I couldn't figure out why so I ploughed on. "I remember we left the sports bar for the big concert in Cardiff Bay after Bayern had scored the first goal. We thought that was it. Then United scored two last-minute goals and they went on to win the treble. Amazing."

"Oh yes," said Zoran, "I remember it alright; 26th of May 1999. How could I forget? That game was going to be the highlight of the season for me. But where was I? Cowering under my bed in a blackout as the British and Americans bombed this city. I couldn't get to a telly to watch it. No-one could."

There was a slight silence. I felt small and embarrassed. Then Zoran laughed, "This bloody country," he said, and raised his glass of Guinness with a shrug.

***

Twelve years later I was back in Belgrade. Chester's degree course in London included a year studying the Serb language at the university and, to get a head start, he'd signed up for one-to-one lessons. We'd had a great weekend 'settling him in' as middle-class parents say. We looked at a couple of flats and walked for hours to get our bearings on the Serbian capital. We drank, talked politics and watched some football. It was just like another one of our trips. We didn't discuss the elephants in the room – my imminent departure and his being left alone in a strange city with a new language to learn and new friends to make. It was as if there was a silent compact between us not to spoil our last precious hours together. Through the three days of beer and bravado, he'd shown just one sign of vulnerability.

"What if I can't hack it here? What if I just don't like it?" he'd said.

Too late. Here I was saying farewell to my boy again at the number 7 tram stop as he trundled off across the River Sava to Novi Beograd and his new life. As we said goodbye I hugged him harder than usual.

"This is your time, Chester," I said. "This will be the best year of your life. Suck every last drop from it. Oh, and write to your mother!" If I had been a real man I would have cried then instead of later on a park bench.

I had a few hours before my flight home and walked aimlessly around the city, my guts churning at the loss of my little boy. I didn't really care that I was lost. No more real ale in Hackney, no more dossing in that dingy basement in Arsenal. Chester was now firmly on his own and far from home. I drifted into Tašmajdan Park and wandered around the cavernous St Mark's Church. It was built in the Serbian medieval style and based on an orthodox monastery near Priština in Kosovo. On one side of the church is the monstrous marble tomb of Emperor Stefan Dušan. He's known as 'The Mighty' and in the 1300s he conquered vast tracts of land and enacted the constitution of the Serbian Empire, known as Dušan's Code.

I sat on a bench in the park trying to take stock, not of Dušan and the legacy of his Greater Serbia, but just stuff. My thoughts were interrupted by a man asking for the time. I knew this because the second time he asked he pointed to his wrist. He was in his late fifties, and had weathered skin. "Я не говорю русский," I replied and immediately felt a fool for telling him I didn't speak Russian. But he understood and quickly put me at my ease. "No problem. You speak English?"

Aleksandar had worked for Barclays Bank in London. "I loved it there. You have a great city. We stayed for ten years, or was it eleven? But you know we just had to come back home." We got on well and walked through the park chatting about children (he had two), politics ("We were never communists, Yugoslavia was a socialist society"), and the European Union (he was not a fan). I instinctively moved away when he touched my elbow and said, "Come with me, I have something to show you." But he gestured kindly, nodding his head towards the other side of the park. It was broad daylight and the ubiquitous snogging Serb teenagers entwined on a bench made me feel safe enough, so I followed him.

"See that," said Aleksandar pointing to a four-storey white building. Next to it was a shiny, new, silvery-blue office block crowned with huge satellite dishes. "That was our television station." The wall on one end of the white building was completely missing, exposing the rooms and floors like an old-fashioned, open-fronted doll's house.

On the 23rd of April 1999, at six minutes past two in the morning, NATO bombed the building of the Serbian Broadcasting Corporation (RTS). Part of the building collapsed. Sixteen people were killed while many were trapped in the wreckage for days. As a reporter, I had liked the way that in conflict, from the Romanian revolution to the Gulf War, the military always targeted TV and radio stations. It gave me, us, the profession, a self-importance. Standing before this, I hated my own vanity.

"That's what your bombs did to us for defending what was ours," said Aleksandar.

'Oh no, not Kosovo,' I thought. I wasn't in the mood for this conversation. But Aleksandar was more pensive than challenging and we both stood in silence before another scar of war.

"Now look over here," he said and pointed to a large slab of rock with lines of Cyrillic script carved into it. It was a memorial to those who had died that night in 1999. Under the heading "зашто?" (Why?) was a list of names. Aleksandar pointed to one of them. It read: "Milan Joksimovich, 47."

"He was my friend," said Aleksandar. "We used to play chess together. We played the night before all this…" His voice trailed off and then he said, "We never finished the game." We shook hands, Aleksandar left and I ran my fingers over the cold stone and down the list of names. I stopped at another name. "Darko Stoimenovski, 25." Just four years older than my Chester. My park bench tears began to feel a little self-indulgent.

On the way to
the Land of Fire

June 2009

AZERBAIJAN. THE LAND of fire where, according to tradition, outside the capital Baku the Iranian prophet Zoroaster built a temple and lit an eternal flame, giving birth to Azeri Zoroastrianism. They say the natural source of the gas at the temple has now been exhausted and the flame is kept alight by a mains pipe. Not so romantic. Two thousand years later this oil-rich former Soviet republic was the birthplace of a rather more prosaic outfit – the Wales football supporters' charity Gôl!

Wales played Azerbaijan in 2002 in a European Championship qualifying match and a group of supporters decided it was time to 'give something back' to the countries we travelled to in support of our national team. We contacted a local charity in Baku and organised a visit to a children's home outside the city with gifts of football kits, clothes, toys and sweets.

Since then Wales fans have visited charities all over Europe. Every time the national team plays, money is raised and the men, women and children who travel away from home do their little bit to show a slightly different side to football fans abroad. Wales seemingly had a love affair with Azerbaijan. The national team were drawn against them three times and played in Baku not only in 2002 but again in 2004 and now in 2009.

The charity visits opened up an exciting, exotic and sometimes disturbing new world for the travelling fans.

***

It was like something from the *The Canterbury Tales*. A latter-day, open-all-hours mediaeval roadside inn. Except this was a modern hotel on the dusty approach to Georgia's second city, Kutaisi. All it seemed were welcome, whatever their state, and never a word was passed in judgement.

The Alaverdi claimed to be a four-star hotel but it was the $22-a-night price tag which had really impressed us. Set off the not-so-busy road we had taken from Trabzon on the Turkish border and through Batumi just inside Georgia, it was a pretty basic two-storey concrete structure. As I passed through the narrow corridor to the dining room, I saw a tubby chef crashed out on a low wooden seat. His head was askew on his shoulder, unshaven jowls crumpled up to his ear, and a filthy apron twisted across his bulging tummy. His assistant was preparing lunch next door in what was no more than a broom cupboard. The door slightly ajar, I peeped in. He was cutting meat on an aged wooden block in a most unbutcherlike fashion with an axe, the pink-red flesh of an uncertain beast being hacked into shapeless chunks.

Kutaisi was our promised land – the place where we finally left the cars which had been our homes for the ten days it had taken us to drive from Cardiff across mainland Europe, and beyond all in aid of Gôl! Our destination again was Azerbaijan. To mark our third visit to the Land of Fire we'd decided to drive there.

The twenty-two men and one brave woman had set off in seven cars, a white Transit van and a London cab packed with supplies for the good causes we were to visit en route. Only six vehicles made it. The black cab didn't get further than Dover, the Transit broke down somewhere south of Nuremberg and the red Vauxhall gave up the ghost and was 'disappeared' by the fans on the Bulgarian-Turkish border. But nothing could stop us. We simply crammed people and kit into the remaining cars and pressed on. Crossing Turkey in two days we made the Georgian border town of Batumi as night fell and on the eleventh day we hit Kutaisi.

Driving 3,500 miles, across fourteen countries, through four time zones was the easy bit. Getting rid of the cars at the end was a little harder. Even though we wanted to donate them to charitable causes, the authorities in Azerbaijan would not allow us to import our second-hand cars. But the Georgians were more amenable. We'd leave the cars there and get a bus into Azerbaijan. Simple. Or so we thought. And that is how we ended up spending several days in Kutaisi's Alaverdi Hotel under house arrest.

***

In the hotel bar a group of young uniformed soldiers had stopped by for an afternoon beer. It was seventy degrees outside and we were all gagging for a drink. A tiny cat ran through the bar and managed to squeeze out of the door before it slammed, shutting out the blinding white sunlight. I may have been tired but the images were sharp, super-real, almost caricatures.

We were served by a waiter who, we later discovered, never slept. He wore black trousers which were shiny on his thighs through wear, a tightly fitting red waistcoat, but no tie. His features were typically Georgian. He had jet black hair and an unkempt moustache. He only had one eye and a slightly crooked back. During our stay he was always on duty, morning, afternoon, through the night and into the early hours, stoically serving the Welshmen (and woman) as they drank, sang and argued about politics and religion, or more likely John Toshack's management style.

We were guests of the Newport–Kutaisi twinning committee and our host was Professor Madonna Megrelishvili, the esteemed and formidable head of English at Kutaisi State

25

University. The beers sunk and the rooms allocated, Professor Megrelishvili formally greeted us in the hotel dining room as we sat down to an extraordinary lunch. The Georgian feast, or 'supra', draws influences from the Middle East and Europe. Soko, mushrooms seasoned with spices and herbs, and khachapuri, fresh bread stuffed with cheese, were stacked high for us. There were small, dry fish, large pieces of the meat I'd seen being cut and piles of fresh green leaves and tomatoes. All this was accompanied by copious amounts of an opaque, greeny-yellow wine, home-made of course.

The formalities over, we presented the cars we had driven from Wales to the charities the twinning committee had chosen – the city's youth football club, the university's English school and intriguingly, the Mayor's office. We had plastered the cars with specially printed stickers naming our sponsors. Our benefactors were as motley as we were – Part Mart, Dial a Weld, the Duke of Clarence pub and Emerald Autoservices of Beccles. We watched the names stripped from the dusty bonnets as the cars were made good for their new lives. Later that week we would see the right-hand drive Rover, Ford and Suzuki being driven by strangers. They looked out of place in a new town, like seeing an ex-girlfriend passing by on the other side of the street, mine but not mine.

Professor Megrelishvili didn't want us to waste a minute and had filled our two days with visits to schools and charities across the city. We'd gained an extra day in Georgia as the visit to Stalin's birthplace at Gori was considered "not safe for you at the moment". Children at the Martve 91 sports school eagerly modelled the old Newport County football kits we had brought, while the students at the university got stuck into the English-language books. There were difficult choices to be made. You are nineteen, maybe twenty. What would you pick? *Harry Potter*, *Jane Eyre* or the 2001 *Shoot* annual?

Duncan, John and I were taken to a specialist music school. As we entered the slightly crumbling but spotlessly clean building I asked our host what the name of the school was.

I thought it might be named after some great son of Kutaisi, a mediaeval king, the composer Borodin or even the former USSR, but still definitely Georgian, foreign minister, Eduard Shevardnadze.

"The name of the school?" came a slightly bemused reply, "Er, number 44."

About half the children were boarders, most of them war refugees or orphans whose families had been killed or displaced when Russia had invaded South Ossetia and Abkhazia, the so-called breakaway Georgian republics, the previous year. The spartan bedrooms were very simply furnished. The scrubbed wooden floor had a threadbare mat. Each child had a narrow bed, a tiny cupboard to call their own and a shared bookcase. But the children took pride in showing us their single teddies and dolls and talked us through the few photos of friends from home they had salvaged and stuck on the wall.

The patriotism of the Georgians is fierce and their pride in their country, language and heritage was never far from the surface. We joined a class of nursery age children who were learning to count.

"The number three is very important to us Georgians," they were told.

As one, the children recited, "One for our country, two for our religion and three for our language." It was a potent mix.

Along the corridor some of the children's drawings had been taped to the peeling wall. They must have been up for some time. There were winter scenes of snowmen and Father Christmas but among them one picture showed an aircraft firing on a village, another a Russian tank rolling through. 'Stop Russia' was crayoned in a child's scrawny hand across the bottom. It was a sobering appeal from kids who were still traumatised by what they had experienced just months earlier. On our way out of the accommodation block in a stairwell we found small graffiti scratched into the wall. It was a simple message. 'Fuck Russia.'

The Georgians pride themselves on their hospitality and

although it was obvious the school did not have two local Lari to rub together, we were served slices of pizza and home-made cake washed down with Georgian champagne and brandy. Our gifts of clothes, toys and sweets were graciously, almost formally, received by the children and staff who made us guests of honour at a special concert. It was an eclectic programme. A doleful violin solo was followed by the youngest lad in the school dressed as a mini Elvis rapping in Georgian. Though they must have heard his song a dozen times before, his classmates clapped and whooped.

"We could be in a school eisteddfod in Bangor," said John Jones, my co-driver on the trip, "only this one has booze, and I am actually enjoying the music!"

A girls' choir sang a traditional song in perfect harmony and the afternoon concert was rounded off with a rousing rendition of the national anthems – theirs and ours. Hands on their little hearts the Georgian children sang with absolute passion, some noticeably louder than the others.

***

The next day we were invited to take part in our very own international game of football. Now not all football supporters are football players. Blame the heat or the Georgian hospitality but we were no match for the students of Kutaisi and we folded five goals to one.

The evening thankfully turned cooler and the wide sky morphed into a smooth salmon pink as we took the steep hill out of town to the Gelati monastery perched above the city. The Church of the Virgin was founded in 1106 by the King of Georgia, affectionately known as David the Builder, and the monastery was for a long time one of the main cultural and intellectual centres in Georgia. As we entered the church, mass was being recited by a group of monks in sober habits. We were the only visitors and looked faintly ridiculous in our football shirts, flip-flops and baggy shorts. We had been driving hard for days and the hushed tones of the age-old scriptures and the cool, damp interior now made us contemplative.

Outside, a giant of an Abbot walked towards us. He had to duck to get through the gothic stone arch as he passed the holy well. Dressed in a heavy black cassock he wore the tall, traditional orthodox priest's stovepipe hat. His beard was full but well kept and he wore the simple adornment of a heavy silver crucifix around his neck. Our guides whispered that our clothes could be a problem for him. I expected the worst so took the initiative.

"Hello," I said as breezily as I could, extending my hand, "what a fantastic place this is. We're from Wales and on our way to Azerbaijan to watch the football."

He grasped my tiny hand, shook it powerfully and gave me a thumping pat on the back. Through the interpreters he welcomed us to the monastery and to Georgia and patiently answered our questions. I asked if we could have our picture taken with him and there was an avalanche of clicks and flashes as he hugged every one of us in turn for the camera. His final words were, "Go to Azerbaijan and smash the infidel," and he let out a big roar of laughter.

***

The visits were done, the cars had been handed over and we were ready to hit the road again. In Tbilisi we were to be guests of honour at the British Embassy. It sounded rather grand. This was to be the last leg of the journey before Azerbaijan. But there was one small problem. At the Turkish border our passports had been stamped to show that we were taking British right-hand drive cars into Georgia. They even wrote the registration number of my Rover on the stamp itself. The border guards on the other side of the country would be expecting us to take the cars out with us. Only we weren't. The cars were now in the possession of the school, university and, hmm, the Mayor's office in Kutaisi. We had a bus waiting to take us out of the

29

city. But the paperwork was not right. Professor Megrelishvili was apologetic, but we were going nowhere.

We raced in taxis like fools around the city in search of a way out, trying solicitors, the police, even the customs and excise people. But the blank faces and shrugged shoulders of the men and women in military style uniforms told me that in this country, stamps are stamps, paperwork is paperwork and we had neither.

The boys began to get nervous as the hours passed at the Alaverdi hotel.

"How are we getting out of here?" asked Dylan, the youth worker from Cardiff.

"*Are* we getting out of here?" asked Rich, the council officer from Conwy. We didn't need an armed guard to keep us penned in. There was nowhere for us to go. An argument started over our next move and the group divided into two camps. Some wanted us to make a break for the border with the bus while the unfortunate drivers, me included, would have to await their fate at the hands of the Georgian authorities.

Dave Jones, the prison officer from Wrexham, towered above the rest of us. He clapped his great hands to get our attention. "Shut up, shut up!" he hollered, "We came here together and we are leaving together." Our immediate fate then was decided, but the Chaucerian experience was now becoming Kafkaesque and how to get out of this Caucasian dream turned nightmare was becoming a real concern.

Enter Professor Megrelishvili and our new friend Mr Nugzar Shamugia, the Mayor of Kutaisi. Thank heavens for that car. We headed back to the police station to assure whoever needed assuring that the offer of these cars was genuine and that they were indeed ours to give away in the first place. Then we had a formal document of exchange drawn up, witnessed by a lawyer and okayed by the customs officials who had previously been so unhelpful. This being a former Soviet society, the form filling was arduous. Everything had to be done in triplicate. Serious-looking men wearing unfeasibly wide-brimmed caps stamped them all. It seemed that the bigger the cap, the more important the official. The Mayor may have wielded considerable clout but the to-ing and fro-ing continued for two days.

Fuelled by the local beer and brandy there was talk of reclaiming the cars and driving them to the Azeri border and dumping them in a ditch. But thankfully the perseverance and connections of Prof Megrelishvili and Mayor Shamugia paid off. The car may have had something to do with it, but who cared? We finally got the news we had been waiting for. The paperwork was complete. The boys sobered up, the bus drove off and despite a broken fan belt twenty miles out of town, we were back on the road to Azerbaijan.

The Horror

June 2009

WE MADE IT to Baku, Wales won the football game and the morning after the night before a small group of us visited a children's home near the Azeri capital. We had done dozens on these visits with Gôl! and they follow a similar pattern. We turn up bleary eyed and bedraggled, have a kick around with the children and make short speeches before handing over our gifts. It may have become formulaic but you know what you are going to get and we know what to do. Not this time.

It was the stench that got you first. Faeces. Human faeces. And there was no escaping it. As we were led through the grim corridors to the classroom, I raised my handkerchief to my nose and mouth to try to keep myself from gagging. Inside, some eighteen children of primary school age sat at benches. Their heads were shaved and they sat silently either side of a long table in ill-fitting and worn clothes. In the corner a television flickered. It showed daytime TV, not a children's channel. Few of the children looked up at these strange visitors despite our bags full of clothes, toys and two trolley-loads of disposable nappies. Some of the kids stared blankly into space. Others rocked back and forth as if comforting themselves, singing a silent song in their heads, a song which no-one else would hear. The old woman in charge, her head wrapped tightly in a patterned headscarf, stood guard and peered warily at us.

The Saray orphanage on the outskirts of the city of Sumqayit lies just twenty miles from Baku but you could not have expected such a contrast to the ostentatious wealth and style of the Azeri capital. Our guides were Konul and Rufat, two locals who wanted to help with our charity work. Konul Azimzade was a twenty-two-year-old graduate. Confident and with impeccable, almost accentless English, she was looking forward to continuing her studies in Germany. Konul was going places.

Rufat was two years her junior and if he had a surname he wasn't telling us. We'd met him on an earlier visit to Azerbaijan. Then he was a street urchin who hung around the city centre bars and cafes, and for a dollar bill he'd tell you the capital of any country in the world. Rufat had graduated in the school of life and was now constantly on his mobile phone cutting his next deal. But today he was our fixer. Konul and Rufat embodied the different faces of modern Azerbaijan. They both spoke Farsi but preferred to use English. Neither seemed at ease here or with each other.

Saray is home to 160 children, most of whom have severe physical and mental disabilities. They suffer from, among other things, cerebral palsy, spina bifida and Down's syndrome.

"We've stopped the physical abuse," said Stefan, the young German doctor who was volunteering at the home for six months. "What I mean is..." He picked up on our shocked reaction.

"Look! You've got to understand the situation here." Stefan pointed to his right. "This woman is in charge of two dozen children, some of them are incontinent, others with real difficulties. How is she supposed to maintain control?" He was right. We knew nothing.

Another woman, in her late fifties, came in and presented a tiny baby to us. He was actually about two years old but his eyes were black and deep-set. His emaciated body was wrapped in a baggy T-shirt. A loincloth, which was once blue but which now looked like a dishrag, was tied around his tiny waist. No nappy. I know how you are supposed to hold a baby, one hand under its bottom and then you cradle its head with your free hand. One of the joys of fatherhood was hugging Chester, my arms making a thick blanket of warm flesh, both of us wrapped in a sweet smelling, powdery love. But with this poor wretch I just couldn't bring myself to do it. There was no "Ahh, baby's had a pooh", as I would have said to baby Chester. There was no hint of Johnson's talc or wet wipes. The stench was days' old. So I picked him up under both armpits. He flew into the air as I miscalculated his weight and there was that smell again, only this time it was even closer.

In a room further down the corridor babies were sleeping, the cots rammed end to end along each side of the dorm in a human battery farm. I looked over into one of them and cooed quietly. A tiny pair of eyes, still sticky with night goo slowly opened and the boy smiled. His little teeth were yellow. I doubted they'd ever been brushed. I waved my hand slowly above his eyes and he followed it. I then touched the stick-like arm and he smiled again. I am convinced that this was the only human interaction the child had had all day. His was the only crib I went to.

Sacha Tomes from the American charity Burnaby Blue visited Saray in 2000, nine years before our visit. This is how she described the place: "A truer representation of Bedlam would be hard to create. On our first visit we saw children carried by an arm and leg to rudimentary baths, for which read a bucket of water. We saw children tied to radiators, others rocking back and forth." Things had changed by the time we visited Saray, but not much.

The older children lived upstairs. On the landing young teenagers lolled in six or seven wheelchairs. Girls and boys sat opposite each other doing... absolutely nothing. One head drooped lowly and the girl emanated a gurgling sound. Spittle ran down her cheek unchecked. Every part of the floor was covered in grey, ripped polythene. "In case of accidents," we were told.

"Do the children get out to play at all?" I asked Stefan whose matter-of-fact, almost breezy, approach to this living hell was becoming more understandable.

"Yes, for an hour or so most days," he said. "But it's difficult to manage so many of them. And what if they tried to get away?"

Azerbaijan is one of the most dynamic economies in the Middle East. American investment in the Caspian Sea's oil fields fuelled growth in GDP of forty per cent in 2007. The capital Baku is one of the wealthiest cities in the region. Along the broad seafront and in the Park Bulvar and Metro Mall you'll find only the best. Armed guards man the Armani and Bulgari stores as besuited visitors glide out through the automatic doors to their shiny black Mercs. But a short ride away, here at the top end of the Absheron peninsula, it's a different story.

Azerbaijan's third city, Sumqayit, has been processing oil since the days of Stalin. The rush to industrialise the Soviet Union took no account of the environment and the people here are living with the legacy. The city was known for its cemetery. They call it Baby Cemetery because it contains so many graves of infants born with deformities. The problems were further complicated by the lack of adequate medical care, especially for the poor.

In 2006 the US-based Blacksmith Institute named Sumqayit the most polluted place on Earth. As well as the oil legacy it has been polluting the local environment with other industrial chemicals, chlorine and heavy metals. Cancer rates here are as much as fifty-one per cent higher than the national average. Genetic mutations and birth defects are commonplace. Disabilities in Azerbaijan are still taboo and some of the children at Saray were dumped on the orphanage's doorstep by parents who couldn't cope.

Stefan told us that there were twenty homes like Saray across Azerbaijan. "It's not so bad here," he said stoically, "but I worry for the kids when they reach eighteen. Then they have to go to adults' homes and the carers there sometimes limit their intake of food and water so that they don't have to clear up after them. Well, you can imagine what happens then." I tried not to.

Azerbaijan hosted the Eurovision Song Contest in 2012. Western countries have courted President Ilham Aliyev and are happy to do business here. Azerbaijan has huge reserves of gas and oil, but the regime is mired in allegations of corruption and vote rigging. Human Rights Watch says political opponents are routinely imprisoned without trial and any journalist who dares speak out is arrested. It's ranked 139th out of 167 in the world for upholding democratic rights. But what about the children of Saray? Don't they have human rights too? And who will speak out for them? What was going on in Saray may be a sin by omission, the hangover of a social and economic system playing catch up with the speed of its new-found wealth. But what I saw in Sumqayit was nothing short of institutionalised state sponsored child abuse.

Charities from across the globe and ex-pat oil workers, Scots and Americans in particular, have done their bit, rebuilding the roof and refurbishing rooms in Saray, but without minimal government intervention and funding nothing will really change. With our gifts of nappies, clothes and footballs we offered a tiny drop of comfort in the filthy, shameful Black Sea. But no more than that.

We travelled back to town along the Sumqayit Highway in our rickety bus in silence. On the city's outskirts we passed the sprawling new international bus terminal. Its uber-modern design makes a bold statement for the Land of Fire. All shiny steel and glass it resembles a massive beached ship. It has a shopping mall of 800 shops, a 500-seat canteen, plush waiting and VIP rooms. It even has its own power station. Rufat broke the silence.

"That's why I hate this fucking country," he said as we stared at the man-made monster. "Look at that! A bus station no-one can get to and shops we can't afford to shop in. That's this country's priorities for you. I can't wait to get out of here."

Konul said nothing. She didn't even look at him. And neither did we.

What's the Basque for 'offside'?

April 2011

"I'M NOT SURE I'd recognise him really," said Josu Amézaga, my guide on my visit through the Basque country, much to my surprise. "I only have a small TV set and the picture's not much good." We were waiting to meet Koikili Lertxundi, Basque football star and Athletic Bilbao's hard-hitting defender, fresh from Sunday night's televised 2–0 defeat of Seville in Spain's La Liga premier division.

The young man in question stepped out of a battered Mercedes van wearing a very plain T-shirt and herringbone Harrington jacket, a mobile phone clutched to his ear. It was not the entrance I was expecting from a professional footballer. Where was the flash car, the designer outfit and the obligatory outsized headphones? But then Koikili is no normal player. We had come to a technology park on the edge of Bilbao to meet him, his father, Jabier, and their six-strong consultancy team which trains football coaches, exclusively in the Basque language.

I'd been doing something similar myself, though I was more of a pub team substitute player than a European superstar. Every Saturday morning for ten years I had paced the side-lines of football pitches across south Wales shouting instructions in Welsh at junior football teams. I was an unlikely, and at first unwilling, recruit. The coach of my son's mini football team was moving back to north Wales. Dylan was blunt, "If you don't take it on, then '*DIM pêl-droed*'." "No football."

They call it the Big Society these days, but I was just doing my bit. The whole point was that these football sessions were the only times the children got to hear and speak Welsh outside school. I had always been hooked on football, but with my new managerial responsibilities now I became a bit of a zealot. One Saturday morning, the freezing sleet started hitting us horizontally at Parc-y-Dwrlyn, a mountain-top pitch north of Cardiff. It was a big game – the Urdd (Welsh youth club) versus Pentyrch Rangers Under 8s. Despite the shocking weather the lads battled on, soaking shirts clinging to their skinny bodies. Jake's mother begged me to call the game off. "No," I said, "It will do them good," and I think we actually won.

As the years went by and the boys turned into youths, the English language started creeping into the training sessions. "*Trwy'r canol!*" and "*Pêl fi!*" became "Through the middle!" and "My ball!" I never made an issue of it, figuring that my not being a teacher but still talking football through Welsh was some sort of example. I was interested to know how coaches in other countries helped normalise a second, minority language. Football is a great way of bringing people together and I was sure it could help young boys and girls see Welsh as an important part of their lives – outside the classroom. Could coaches like me in Wales learn from the experience of others? The European Union used to be quite keen on promoting minority, indigenous languages so I applied for a grant to study how my Basque counterparts went about things. And that's how I ended up on a windswept training ground outside Bilbao talking to a professional footballer.

More than 600,000 people speak Basque, or *Euskara*, across the northernmost provinces of Spain and into France. Following decades of decline, the language is making something of a comeback. Many schools teach all their lessons exclusively through the medium of Basque. There are Basque-language television and radio stations and a newspaper. It predates all other Indo European languages and to outsiders it's an impenetrable tongue. Basque is not related to any other language and with its juxtaposition of the letters X, Z and K, it must be a Scrabble player's dream. Or nightmare.

As we drove to meet Koikili, I was briefly transported back to the road signs protests in Wales during the 1970s when campaigners used to daub the English-only version of traditionally Welsh place-names with green paint. The Basque name for Bilbao is Bilbo. There's no A in it and campaigners had painted out the A on many a road sign along the main road. This is a passionately nationalistic country which has seen an armed struggle with the Spanish authorities in faraway Madrid. The ETA terrorist group, which has been fighting for full political independence, had only recently put down its arms.

Now, the people of the Basque country are seeking self-determination through purely democratic means. The culture is cherished and supported by most people, regardless of which language they speak. The parallels with Wales and the Welsh language are clear. Koikili explained how the Basque schools are turning out a new generation of speakers, but that the children don't get the chance to speak the language in social settings outside school. His mission is to train a different breed of coaches who make Basque the first language of play in this football-obsessed nation. "It's all a matter of commitment," he said as he explained how he personally puts in up to six hours a day, after his professional training sessions, to nurture young players and coaches. This put my Saturday morning volunteering on Llandaff Fields into perspective.

In my faltering Spanish I asked how many of his fellow professionals at Athletic Bilbao had second jobs like this. Koikili answered in Basque through Josu, "None," he said, "but they are happy to give up some of their time to help us." The Athletic Bilbao club is supportive too, providing balls and equipment for the training sessions.

Since 1912 Athletic has followed a strict unwritten rule

of only fielding Basque players, although recently a few non-Basque players have been recruited to play for Los Leones (The Lions). Their favourite saying, and I have to quote it in Spanish here, is: *"Con cantera y afición, no hace falta importación* – With home-grown talent and local support, you don't need foreigners."* I can't see Cardiff City surviving long in British football's pyramid system if they followed a similar policy, but that was the only lesson from Bilbao that I chose to forget.

From his dad's offices we followed Koikili in the old Merc van for twenty minutes to a training ground at the village of Sondika. The lush training pitch backed right up to the airport runway and I ducked as a plane took off, its undercarriage almost scraping the goalposts. The Sondika club runs eight football teams across all age groups. As we arrived, two teams of twelve year olds were being put through their paces. *"Kaixo, kaixo,"* said Koikili, greeting everyone in Basque. The TV cameras had arrived and there was a photographer from the Spanish-language Basque paper *Mundo Deportivo*, all keen to get a piece of the player.

The children seemed a little nervous as he walked onto the pitch. Already old enough to know it wasn't cool to be star-struck, they nonetheless threw sly glances towards their footballing hero, especially after they had scored a goal or had dribbled the ball around an opponent.

We had come to see an assessment session, not for the children, but for Koikili's coaches. The checklist was familiar to me: preparation, equipment, technique, feedback to players, any questions? But top of Koikili's list was the use of the Basque language by the coaches and how the children responded. It was no surprise that they all passed with flying colours.

"The coaches must show commitment," said Koikili, "and the children too. We can help them see that the Basque language belongs to them all and actually offers them an advantage on the pitch. It gives them that extra strength. It's a unique and powerful bond."

I had said something similar to the shivering kids in Cardiff many times on those long lost Saturday mornings. But to hear someone else, and a real life professional footballer to boot, singing the same hymn (even if I couldn't understand his words) was both a revelation and vindication. In the short time we'd been together, Koikili and I had formed our own bond of understanding. We both believed in the power of football as a single international language to help preserve and promote our very different tongues.

Back at the offices on the technology park I noticed some impressive academic certificates framed on the wall of Jabier Lertxundi's office. Koikili's dad had a degree in sociology and a PhD in economics from the University of the Basque Country.

"He got the first of those while he was in prison," said my guide Josu, casually.

"Prison?" I said, a little taken aback. Smartly turned out in his well-ordered offices Jabier looked every inch the dynamic European entrepreneur.

"Yes," answered Josu. "He was arrested in 1987, tortured, and sentenced to twelve years in prison for allegedly helping members of ETA escape from custody."

I could now see where the no-nonsense professional footballer, at the top of his game, got his drive to promote all things Basque. Commitment, as Koikili himself might have said.

One of us –
the death of Mikey Dye

September 2011

I WASN'T EXPECTING much, to be honest. It may have been England versus Wales at Wembley but the Welsh side had already lost to the 'old enemy' in Cardiff and a few other teams along the way, leaving us no real hope of reaching the finals of the 2012 European Championship. Any thoughts of a month in Poland and Ukraine following our team were long-distant memories. Such has been the burden of Wales football fans through the years. Well, since 1958 anyway when we last qualified for the World Cup, and that's well before my time.

There was the Anglo-Welsh rivalry I suppose. When the draw was made, my football buddy John had said, "They'll never allow it. There'll be fighting all the way down Wembley Way. You know how idiotically anti-English some of the lads are." But the game went ahead and the day itself had started off rather promisingly.

Chester and I had played in a friendly match that afternoon and received a genuine welcome at Wealdstone FC. (I am not sure whether it is odd or pathetic for a man in his fifties to play football in the same team as his eighteen-year-old son but hey, while I still can, I will.) These fans' matches had become a regular feature on our international travels and the Wales Supporters' team has played, and more often than not lost, all over Europe from Russia to Iceland, Latvia to San Marino.

At Wealdstone the English had scored a disputed goal in

the last minute to tie the match at full-time. Chester received a yellow card for his undiplomatic questioning of the referee's pedigree but we went on to win on penalties and there was much celebration and merriment in the clubhouse. There was even a winners' cup to mark the occasion and our captain, Dave O'Gorman, dutifully filled it up with of all things, cider and Red Bull. It's not often Wales win at anything let alone against England. Old enemies? Not that afternoon as we drank, sang and made new friends in the London borough of Harrow.

Come six o'clock we were a little worse for wear as we made our way to the game. "Watch your backs lads and stick with us," said our new friends protectively as they marched us from the Tube and down Wembley Way. It was all so good natured, a true celebration of friendship and football.

But as we neared the ground we could see police and paramedics on the concourse encircling something, someone. Definitely someone. Yes, someone was lying flat on his back being treated on the ground. "Probably a drunk," I told Chester dismissively, and with a little contempt for someone who appeared to have stained the reputation of the Wales fans, we made our way inside the stadium to our seats.

I could sense there was something seriously wrong at half-time. Andy, the Welshman from Reading, told me that a supporter had been attacked outside the ground and left unconscious. "One of ours. It didn't look good, Tim," was his judgement. But as we waited in our bus with the sad floodlights dimming from inside Wembley after the inevitable defeat, we heard the news no supporter ever wants to hear. A fan, a man about my age, had been hit by a single punch. He'd fallen hard on the floor. He was dead.

The mobile phones went into overdrive. Rumours abounded through text messages, on Twitter and on Facebook. It was a gang of English fans looking for a fight. No, Swansea City's lads had attacked their rivals from Cardiff. Five men, one punch. It didn't really matter because amid the chatter and noise one thing was painfully clear. Mikey Dye, a Cardiff fan like me, a father like me, a man who I had seen countless times supporting the City and Wales, a football fanatic, a regular guy – was dead.

The following Saturday Cardiff played Doncaster at our shiny new stadium. For once the buzz of expectation as we made our way to the ground was missing. Today it seemed that everyone was talking in hushed tones. We were walking more slowly, more deliberately. As we reached the old Ninian Park gates, which offer an almost ceremonial entrance to the new stadium, a blanket of wreaths, club shirts and Cardiff and Wales flags was laid out to remember Mikey Dye.

Tributes were paid to him over the public address system that afternoon and the announcer also mentioned the passing of the father of the Swansea City manager, Brendan Rogers. There was none of the usual anti-Swansea chanting and there was a minute's silence before the kick-off to remember both men. Silence drowning out the enmity between clubs or between countries. A silence to help us remember that we are each one of us fans.

The mindless acts of individuals or groups will never stop me from following football. At that Cardiff match one supporter suggested this single death could be a turning point and that the hooligans who have caused mayhem for years would finally see that they were playing with real lives. I'm not so naïve as to believe that, but I am sure that Mikey's death was something of a wake-up call to more than one of the "faces" who follow Cardiff, the thugs and yobs who target other supporters "because they're Swansea". Or Millwall or Leeds or any other unfortunate fan who happens to support the wrong team that day.

As I write this I am preparing to go to Swansea to watch Wales play Switzerland before travelling to Bulgaria. These are Wales's last games in yet another depressing and failed attempt to qualify for the finals of a major football championship. In some bar in Sofia or hopefully with a crowd of Swansea fans at the Liberty Stadium I'll raise a glass to one who won't be there.

However, I will have one regret this international weekend. I won't be able to play myself on Sunday afternoon at the tiny Bryntirion ground in Bridgend. No, by then I'll be well on my way to Eastern Europe. But this match is probably the most important of them all. It's a game to commemorate the life of Mikey Dye and to raise money for his family. It's another supporters' match, but this time it's between Cardiff and Swansea. All enmities between these rival clubs will be buried as we remember one of us.

Playing for peace in Kenya

November 2011

NEVER MIND THE sectarian rivalry of Celtic versus Rangers. At election time in Kenya supporting the wrong football team can cost you your life.

Stabua Khatija Yusuf lives in Nairobi's most notorious district. The Kibera slum is home to some 200,000 men, women and children. No-one is quite sure how many. From a distance Kibera forms a sprawling patchwork quilt of reddish-brown shacks, all topped with rusting corrugated iron roofs. They say that if you're not from Kibera then don't go in there without a local by your side, as you will never find your way out of the maze of connecting streets.

Stabua is twenty-one and combines her university studies with coaching the Anyany Sisters women's football team. Many of the girls who play for Anyany are victims of rape and domestic sexual abuse. Some of the rapes were politically motivated, carried out during the violence that claimed hundreds of lives following Kenya's disputed presidential election in 2007. Stabua doesn't actually like football. She told me that she started the girls' team during the school holidays to try to help the rape victims, some of whom are as young as twelve, regain their self-respect. "Of course the facilities are poor here," she says, "we don't even have a full kit half the time, but the girls love playing football and it really has made a difference to them." Unlike most of the other people I met in Kenya, Stabua needed some encouragement to speak to me though she said very little about herself or why she was personally committing so much to this particular cause. I didn't press her.

Hers was just one of many stories I heard during a week working for the British Council with youth and community leaders from across Kenya. Our goal was to help build social cohesion and try to prevent inter community and political violence in the run-up to the 2012 presidential election. Like everyone else in Kenya, Stabua and the Anyany Sisters are the victims of their country's recent history.

In December 2007 President Mwai Kibaki was declared the winner of the presidential election. Kibaki's opponent, Raila Odinga, cried foul, saying that the election was rigged. All hell broke loose. Opposition supporters went on the rampage across the country, most notably in Odinga's homeland of Nyanza Province as well as the slums of Nairobi. Police shot a number of demonstrators and ethnic violence escalated. The madness peaked with the killing of thirty unarmed civilians in a church on New Year's Day 2008. As the country faced the prospect of civil war, the two opposing candidates put their differences aside, formed a coalition government and vowed to do everything in their power to maintain peace.

Since then the British Council has been working with groups calling themselves Active Citizens across Kenya to help build social cohesion. The idea is that by promoting sporting, environmental and social projects, anything in fact which excites and enthuses people, we can improve relations between communities.

A group of Kenyans visited Britain in 2009 and were impressed with the way we had been using sport to build the confidence of young people. They saw Cardiff City's Football in the Community team developing young players and coaches at schools in the poorer areas of the city. Many of these boys and girls had been written off by the system but by using something they were all interested in, football, they were growing educationally and socially. Two years later we were invited back to Kenya to again put those Active Citizens we had met in Cardiff through their paces both on and off the pitch.

Upper Hill High School sits about a mile out of town on the potholed road which winds down to central Nairobi. It's a ramshackle collection of single-storey buildings, all painted a dull, uniform yellow. Upper Hill High prides itself on its academic excellence and the walls of the cramped library, which was to be our home for the week, were packed with well-thumbed books. African short stories backed onto English and maths textbooks. There was a smaller section with books written in the indigenous language Kiswahili. It was an eclectic collection. *Ants Observed* lay back to back with a throwback to colonial times, *The Story of Rhodesia and Nyasaland*.

It was the school holidays but one lunchtime I saw a group of young boys milling around the main building. This lot weren't kicking a ball against a wall. They stood in small circles, colourful towels wrapped around their waists which they were holding out in front of themselves as if to let the air in. One of my colleagues Olga asked me what was going on. I thought they may have come from a swimming lesson and were playing at some silly game airing themselves down below. I was partly right. They had all been circumcised that morning and were holding the towels out to numb the pain. At the end of the week I rather nervously asked the Kenyan men in our group about it. They sniggered at my embarrassment. "What? You've not been cut? You really should," said our man from the government and they laughed like drains.

Circumcision Day was just one of a number of cultural lessons that I was taught during my time in Kenya. My PowerPoint presentation was projected onto a dusty sheet pegged to a line across the library. "Today I want to talk about communication," I said. I had been touted as some sort of expert and was desperate not to sound pompous. "When you're organising a tournament or social event you'll need to be wary of Facebook groups and Twitter. People say they will attend your event online and then never turn up." I asked the class what was the one thing they needed to make sure the message was getting out. Someone said posters in public buildings, another said they would use word of mouth.

Then one young man raised his hand. "A loudspeaker," he said. "What I really want is a loudspeaker so that I can tell everyone on market day what we are doing."

So much for Twitter and Facebook. So much for sharing my expertise.

We gave the Active Citizens at Upper Hill a week of practical coaching and showed them how to organise clubs and tournaments. Together we discussed how we could use sport to bridge religious and ethnic divisions. Everyone in the class had a story to tell.

"Call me Scaar. Yes, that's my nickname. Scaar," said Oscar Omondi Onyango. "It's what they call me back home in the Nyanza Province."

Nyanza. Odinga. I instantly made the connection between the place and the country's opposition leader. Softly spoken, with thin-rimmed glasses and sporting a smart pink shirt, Scaar looked like a rising academic or IT consultant. But he described himself as a "community mobiliser" who for years had witnessed how the families of Nyakach District had suffered from cattle rustling. Young men from the Kalenjin tribe cross the river Miriu and make off with the cattle of the Luo people. Tit-for-tat raids have left many dead and the homes of suspected rustlers are regularly torched.

It had to stop. So Scaar organised a cross-community football festival to "sensitise" young men as he put it, to the consequences of their actions. "Of course the politicians care," he said with a little smile. "They care enough to sponsor football trophies and competitions alright, and even buy kits for the winning team. But it's their name on the trophy and it's all organised by their own families. The day after polling, they're gone, never to be seen again. It's not just in Nyakach. It's the same all over Kenya." Heads across the classroom nodded knowingly.

Scaar is looking for a longer lasting fix to his region's problem and listened attentively as Mizan Rahman talked about the multicultural league he had set up in south Wales. Religious observance, driving taxis or working late in restaurants means young men from ethnic backgrounds in Cardiff or Swansea simply cannot commit to Friday evenings or Saturday afternoons, when most league football games are played. So Mizan arranged for Pakistani, Somali and other black, Asian and minority ethnic teams to play in a league of their own not bound by traditional kick-off times. It has proved a big success and rather than ghettoising these players, when they can, the Yemeni team, and the All Stars, who come from the Bangladeshi community, play in the regular local Sunday league.

The violence in Kenya escalates at election time and farmers on both sides of the river Miriu were dreading the presidential poll. But Scaar is convinced he can emulate the success of the Welsh multicultural league. "If we can get the village elders to support this and speak to the young men during the tournament," he said, "we can get a real dialogue going between the tribes. It's got to be worth a try."

The day's training over, we flew south to Mombasa and drove for forty-five minutes to Diani. This is where most tourists visiting Kenya hit the beach in five-star luxury. The brilliant white sands of the Indian Ocean are studded with tasteful air-conditioned holiday complexes, complete with landscaped coconut groves and water features. All are gated communities. We, however, were in the spartan Diani Community Centre which is set back a little from the dusty main coast road. Our hosts were Mary, Jean and Bakari, who had all visited Wales in 2009 and who were now putting into practice some of what they had seen.

Mary was encouraging Muslim women who had never had a job to seek some form of employment. Making jewellery at home from beads and polished coconut shells to sell to tourists was particularly popular. It brought in much needed cash and posed no threat to the husband's standing as the primary bread winner. Jane, meanwhile, had been recruiting young men to collect leaves in massive paper bags. They store them for a year and then sell them as compost. These micro businesses are both environmentally friendly and offer some hope to the young men and women of Diani.

Bakari organised a cross-community football tournament ahead of the previous year's referendum on Kenya's new constitution. The Digo tribe is in the majority down here, but being a cosmopolitan area there are many conflicting traditions and communities, each vying for influence and power. Bakari had managed to get twenty teams from different areas along the coastal strip to play on the threadbare local ground. Speeches urging youths not to fight were made by local elders and politicians between the games. It may have been a coincidence but the referendum passed here without any serious incident.

The passion and commitment of the young Kenyans to try to change things was again demonstrated by Daniel Onyancha from Rongo in western Kenya. He has been coaching football for many years but disaster struck in a junior game. His neighbour's son broke his leg in a heavy tackle. It was a bad break and the bone had to be reset. Daniel took the boy to hospital for treatment but the lad's mother later demanded 750,000 Kenyan shillings (about £5,000) to pay the hospital bills. With no insurance things were looking bleak for Daniel. He ended up having to sell part of his family's land in order to pay the bill. "I thought of giving up the football. Really I did. But what else would I do?" he said.

There were two elections looming in Kenya, the parliamentary as well as the big one, the presidential election. There would be little to choose between the candidates. Elections here are not fought as in Britain on traditional, ideological grounds. Individual politicians wield great influence and in their regions will promise new roads and bridges or some other targeted populist investment in return for votes. That has the potential to set one area against another. Allegations of favouritism to one community or tribe abound.

The arguments had started already with the government itself demanding the election be put back until the end of the year. This time voters would have to produce biometric identity cards before casting their votes, in an attempt to ensure a free and fair election. Would the Kenyan Active Citizens and their belief in the power of sport and community be able to influence anything on the ground and ensure some semblance of normality, whoever won the election? I didn't know. But if the election were to have been fought on the basis of commitment and goodwill, then Stabua, Scaar, Daniel, in fact any one of them, would certainly get my vote.

***

The fears of violence persisted and the 2012 presidential election was, as predicted by many, delayed, but just a few months later the polls opened. Kenyans turned out in large numbers. Eighty per cent of registered voters came out to vote. There were no serious incidences of violence and the electoral process was deemed by international observes as free, fair and credible.

On top of the world

March 2012

I DON'T THINK I'd ever seen a reindeer before. Well, not like this one anyway. The Sámi herdsman's lasso had caught the beast's right antler and torn it off, leaving tiny specks of blood in the snow. The grey reindeer ran out of control in angry circles, his eyes bulging, bucking and shaking his head wildly. I backed away fearing Santa's little helper was about to turn nasty but was reassured by the young herdsman. "It's OK," he said, "that happens sometimes. He'll calm down in a minute." Thankfully, he did.

The never-ending tundra outside the tiny town of Kautokeino in northern Norway was starkly beautiful. The lake had been frozen solid all winter and was covered in thick virgin snow. For five weeks of summer the sun doesn't set here and for six weeks in the winter the sun doesn't rise. But it was March now, clear as a crystal though sharp as a knife and we stood under a sparkling white sky. The hills were some way off and I felt slightly vulnerable in this vast, bleak and alien landscape.

I had come to Kautokeino, two hundred miles inside the Arctic Circle, to attend the conference of the grandly named World Indigenous Television Broadcasters Network. I had read about the Sámi people and their semi-nomadic lifestyle and my hosts were very keen to share their culture with me. As I was driven out of the town we passed herds of wild reindeer snuffling through the snow in search of whatever they could find below the surface. We stopped at a tiny village camp which had been set up just off the road. Four or five lavvus, the traditional Sámi reindeer skin tipis, had been raised in a semi-circle and the hamlet was busy with much to-ing and fro-ing between the tents.

Wood smoke rose in a straight line from the top of the lavvus and when it wafted out of the front flaps it hit you smack in the face. "Your clothes will smell of this for days," said Nils Johann Hætta who, when not organising visits like this, is head of the Sámi television news service in nearby Karasjok. "I love it," he said. "It smells of, oh I don't know, home."

Nils explained to me that Kautokeino, or Guovdageaidnu as it is known in the Sámi language, is home to 3,000 people. And 100,000 reindeer. "Of course we don't all live like this any more," he said, "but we make a point of trying to pass our customs and traditions on to the next generation."

Sápmi (that's the name for the nation as opposed to the language itself), encompasses parts of the far north of Sweden, Norway, Finland and the Kola Peninsula of Russia. The Sámi people are involved in fishing, fur trapping, and farming but they are best-known as reindeer herders. Of the 80,000 Sámi people only some 3,000 are involved full-time herding. Today their economy has diversified, new people have moved in and the Sámi traditions and their different languages are dying out.

I lifted the flap and ventured into one of the lavvus. Three women were busy cooking. They were all wearing the striking blue national costume with thin, braided, red and white fringes flowing down from the yolk. Tight hats covered their ears and enormous shiny metal pendants hung on their chests. The two older women were showing the younger one, their granddaughter maybe, how to prepare reindeer meat and offal in a massive pot over a hissing gas stove. I was invited to sit cross-legged before the pungent wood fire in the centre of the tent. Nils and I were handed wooden cups of steaming reindeer broth. He took a sip and smiled as he checked his iPhone. "We don't use the stars any more," he laughed. "When we follow the reindeer now we use GPS and the internet to track their migration."

The Sámis are harnessing new technology while trying to hold on to the old ways. Like the women Nils too was decked out in traditional dress. His was a fabulous green costume adorned with gold braiding and intricate red and blue stitching. He wore stout reindeer boots and the obligatory hat. But he'd arrived at camp on a shiny black motorised Skidoo.

That night Nils invited me to his house for dinner. His single-storey home was the height of Nordic chic, plenty of space, floor to ceiling windows, polished wood floors and lots of candles. He served roast reindeer and a glass of aquavit, the local fire water. Nils and his family speak Davvisámegiella, one of the nine closely related Sámi languages. Some of these languages have already died out and there are only 15,000 speakers of this northern dialect left. Nils fears his could be the last generation to speak it.

History has not been too kind to his people. Over the years there has been in-migration and disputes over water, grazing and land rights. As far back as 1852 the 'Kautokeino Uprising' saw the town revolt and attack representatives of the Norwegian authorities. The rebels killed the local merchant and government official, whipped their servants and the village priest, and burned down the merchant's house. One of the ringleaders, a certain Aslak Hætta, was later executed by the Norwegian government. Nils told me he was a 'very distant' relative of his.

After years of discrimination though, the Sámi are fighting back. In the 1970s and '80s the Norwegian government wanted to build a hydroelectric power plant across the Alta river on traditional Sámi lands. There were mass protests and the Alta Controversy became a rallying point for all Sámi people. It focused national attention not only on the environmental damage the barrage would cause, but also on the wider issue of Sámi civil rights. Things started to change. A Sámi national anthem and flag were created. In certain regions of the Nordic countries reindeer herding was legally reserved only for Sámi people. There's now a Sámi University College and an impressive Reindeer Husbandry Institute right here in Kautokeino and in 1989 the first elections were held for the Sámediggi, the Sámi parliament.

"We've fought really hard for the Sámi people and the language," said Nils. "We have TV and radio, lots of publications, newspapers and all that. We even have the Sámi parliament. But it's no good. It's the same as with all the other small languages. The kids move to the cities looking for work, the older people are dying off and the language just isn't being passed on to the children."

After dinner Nils's daughter, Máddji, stood in the middle of the living room and cleared her throat. She had long hair, was heavily pregnant and radiated the good health of a mum-to-be. Her boyfriend, Runi, looked on adoringly. "I want to sing to you my *joik*," she said. A *joik* is a deeply personal or spiritual Sámi folk song and can be dedicated to a person, an animal or just to a certain special place. The song has just a few words that are repeated over and over. Sometimes there are no words at all, just a sound. Máddji is a singer of some renown and has recorded an album called *Dobbelis* (Beyond). Nils helped her write the lyrics. "This *joik* was given to my great-uncle. It's his and his alone," said Máddji, "but I can share it with you." And then she joiked. It was a fantastic ululation. I have no idea what she was saying but it was an uplifting chant, similar to a round. We all applauded. Nils beamed.

I thanked Nils for welcoming me into his family home and as I headed out into the freezing night I asked about Máddji and Runi.

"Is he a local?" I said.

"Yes. Sort of," said Nils rather cagily. "He's from southern Norway."

"Erm, does he speak Sami too?" I ventured.

"Not yet," said Nils, "but he's learning. Oh yes, he's learning."

This club belongs to me and thousands of others like me

February 2013

THE NIGHT WE played Brighton was one of the coldest nights of the year. So to warm us up our owner Vincent Tan gave every supporter a red scarf. Nice gesture? Or a cynical attempt to finally paint the Bluebirds his lucky red? In the face of opposition from us the fans, the billionaire Malaysian had rebranded Cardiff City Football Club. Out went a hundred years of tradition, the blue shirts became red and the club symbol, the Bluebird, was replaced by a dragon, 'to show the fusion of Welsh and Malaysian cultures'.

The scarf giveaway was the last straw for Chester, who was just nineteen. One look at the stadium, thousands of his fellow fans wrapped in free red scarves, and he was off, never to return. It split us as a family. Helen and I had taken him to watch 'the City' as a babe in arms. His room was a shrine to players present and past. We even arranged our family holidays around the pre-season friendlies. Not any more. That night Chester texted me from the Butcher's Arms at full-time. "How did *your* club get on?" It was a taunt, and it hurt.

Vincent Tan had polarised the supporters. His style was, well, idiosyncratic. He had allegedly signed players without the manager's knowledge and tried to dictate playing tactics.

Earlier in the year he had undermined the manager, Malky Mackay, by dismissing Iain Moody, the club's successful head of recruitment. And let's not forget the controversial rebrand, brought in without any consultation with fans or supporters' groups. Many of us felt sidelined, our feelings ignored. Some things at a football club are sacred. You may own a listed building but society says you can't do with it what you want. That's how we all saw 'the City'.

Tan had invested heavily in the club (albeit through loans attracting seven per cent interest) and, by the hard work of Mackay and his players, ultimately delivered Premier League football to Cardiff for the first time in fifty years. But the ultimatum to Malky in an email to 'walk or get sacked' finished it for many supporters. There were protests at the stadium and a number of fans simply handed in their season tickets.

It is not so much what Tan did but the way he went about it. Despite several requests I have only met Tan Sri Vincent Tan, to give him his full honorific Malaysian title, twice, and then only by chance. The first time was at a reception in London to celebrate our promotion to the Premier League. Malky Mackay was there too. It was a night of smiles and handshakes. I cornered Mr Tan.

"You could be the greatest man in this club's history," I told him, "just compromise with us on the colours." But Tan was not for turning.

"Find yourself a new owner," he said sharply, "and convince him."

So why do we all still go 'down the City?' Why do supporters put up with being ignored by clubs and treated like fools? Because, put simply, whichever millionaire's name is on the deeds, Cardiff City actually belongs to me and thousands of other supporters like me. It is part of my family and my community. It has a tradition and heritage that goes way beyond the match-day experience and we will be here long after Vincent Tan has gone.

Fans are not going to go away and their voice should be

heard. We in Cardiff look with envy down the M4 at our rivals in Swansea. That football club has a local chairman and the supporters' trust has a twenty per cent shareholding in the club as well as a representative on the board of directors. The fans' voice in Swansea is heard loud and clear. This is how it should be. While at Cardiff we may be banging our head against a brick wall, we still must believe.

Football is not a business and I am not a customer. Call me a romantic and a fool but I will continue to follow the "Bluebirds" as I have done for twenty-something years. Because no-one, no-one, can take this club away from me.

OK, so we got promoted and for many fans the change to playing in red was a price worth paying for place at the top table. Chester and his crowd had made their choice too. Others, Helen and I included, would forgive for now but never forget what one man had done to our club, our family. We kept the faith and joined the other supporters in line for the promotion party. The Blues were going up!

***

The rear door of the new Bentley swung open and a short, dapper man with shiny silver hair stepped out into the bright light of a spring evening. This was a scene I never thought I would witness. Our nemesis, Sam Hammam, the Lebanese businessman who drove my club to the brink of extinction, who'd run up debts numbered in millions, stepping out in front of the main reception of Cardiff City Football Club. Surely he wouldn't have the face to attend our end of season knees-up? After we had gained promotion to the Premier League, in spite of him? But then came a voice from the other side of the car.

"Sam! Sam!" shouted the Malaysian man who was also dressed as if he'd spent the afternoon at a wedding. "Stay there. I'm coming now." And with that the billionaire Vincent Tan and our former chairman, sped off to the city leaving us faithful Bluebirds standing in line for our promotion party. Welcome to the divided world of modern football.

For years Cardiff City was an 'also ran' in the football stakes. There had been the odd promotion of course, closely followed by the inevitable drop back down a division, and yes that one FA Cup win in 1927, but nothing really since then. For generations we'd paid to stand on the Bob Bank (so-called because it only cost a shilling, a 'bob', to get in), in the hope of seeing the Bluebirds fly. Even flap a bit. But they never did.

How things had changed. With a little investment and a lot more luck we had hit the jackpot. We'd won promotion and were the newest members, for a year at least, of the world's wealthiest football 'club', the Premier League. Or should I say the Barclays Premier League® as we must now call it. Things had moved on apace. Mr Tan had struck a deal with his new friend Sam to settle his debts and had bestowed on him the title Life President of the Club for good measure.

Cardiff then, had followed the same path as other successful English clubs. You see, it is businessmen, foreign businessmen usually, who now call the shots in the Premier League, not the cloth cap brigade. Funny regional accents have been replaced by different voices, some of them requiring an interpreter to be heard on *Match of the Day*. There's the Glazer family at Man U (Americans), Roman Abramovich at Chelsea (Russian) and Sheikh Mansour the owner of Man City (Abu Dhabi.) Thanks to their generosity the world has been scoured and the very best players from Mali to Korea (though not the North, you understand) now grace the hallowed turf of Old Trafford and Stamford Bridge. Everybody happy? Well no, not everybody, as it happens.

A lot of supporters are concerned that the latest must-have toy for wealthy industrialists is a football club. Got the yacht, personal jet and a billion in the bank? What next, chaps? I know, how about buying a football club? It sounds tempting but this financial model of private and personal ownership is totally unsustainable and threatens the critical link between clubs and the communities which created, and which still, just, sustains them.

Our big football clubs survive on the back of massive financial debt and can only service the interest on those debts because of the constant flow of television monies. An owner will spend vast sums enticing the best players to his club. To compete at this level the next team must do the same. The argument runs that this expenditure shows the club and the owner's 'ambition'. But what it actually does is create an upward spiral of wage inflation and a vicious circle of spend, success, debt and more spending. The only real winners are the players and their agents who can command eye-watering sums in transfer payments, fees, sell-on clauses and bonuses.

Since the Premier League was established in 1992 no fewer than seventy professional football clubs have faced insolvency. Between 2001 and 2006, ninety-two clubs announced pre-tax losses of £1,014million. So what happens when Uncle Sam or the Venky brothers (the Indians who bought Blackburn Rovers) lose interest or the club underperforms and drops down a division or two? Sell up? Find some other interest? And to hell with the fans?

This is a real danger. According to a report by the international accounting group BDO in 2013, sixty-five per cent of English and Welsh clubs were wholly dependent on their main sponsor to pay off their debts. In the lower divisions a third of club owners were considering selling up. All this despite the financial fair play rules introduced by UEFA which are supposed to rationalise every club's expenditure and income.

At the same time the beautiful game is becoming estranged from its roots and the diehard fans who support their team come what may. Ticket prices have rocketed, shutting out much of the traditional fan base. Going to watch Arsenal or 'MU' as the marketeers call them, is now an event, like a visit to the opera. In the cheap(er) seats at pitchside, Japanese tourists clicking away at every throw-in seem to have replaced father and son with their half-time flask of sweet tea. Yep, business is business and if you don't like it, tough. But does it have to be like this?

They take a very different view of things in Germany. There the local communities own fifty per cent plus one of the shares of every football club. The Bundesliga has strict financial rules and important decisions about the club are made by the members of the club in the interests of the club, not those of an outside investor. No club in Germany has gone to the wall, they have bigger crowds, the clubs are closer to the communities they serve, more players choose to stay in their own country and ticket prices are lower. German teams regularly contest the European Champions League final and according to FIFA, Germany is consistently ranked one of the best teams in the world. It's a similar story in Spain. In Brazil, only clubs in the lower divisions are owned by individual investors. Teams like Santos, São Paulo and Vasco da Gama are all in the hands of local people.

It appears that local ownership by fans actually works. So what are the prospects nearer home? With the help of an organisation called Supporters Direct more than thirty football clubs are now owned by fans including Portsmouth, AFC Wimbledon, Newport County and Exeter City. This small organisation promotes sustainable sports clubs based on community ownership and rejects the traditional business model of private ownership which puts clubs at risk of short-term vested interests, poor financial management and inadequate governance. It believes that democratic supporter involvement can help redress this imbalance. Supporters Direct started off serving only British football but it now works in more than twenty European countries.

So let's welcome the millions of Messrs Tan and Hammam. And all the best to Cardiff, who inevitably dropped out of football's top flight after a single season. But remember that Vincent Tan has already threatened to leave the club if he is not 'shown respect'. Yes, we welcome them all and give them thanks. But Vincent, who will be here in a hundred years' time?

The second time I met Mr Tan I almost got to ask him that very question. Almost, but it was not to be. Here's why.

"Any other business?" asked Mehmet Dalman, the dapper club chairman and, as if on cue, the boardroom door swung open. Our 'fans representatives' meeting was really over but there was one last surprise. In the doorway, flanked by three Malaysians with shaved heads was Vincent Tan.

"Sorry I'm late but I said I would try to get here. Traffic around Swindon. You know how it is," he said with a broad smile. Mr Tan entered the room leaving his minders behind the closed door. Was this the long-awaited meeting with supporters? Goodness knows we had been trying to speak to him for years but had been fobbed off with chairmen, chief executives and ground staff. Tan had flatly refused to meet his critics, the very supporters on whom his club depended. This sudden appearance took us all by surprise. We'd been ambushed. One-nil to the club.

Vincent Tan may be the major shareholder of our football club but we refuse to call him our owner as we believe that we, the fans, are the true owners and guardians of Cardiff City. Mr Tan's formal title, Tan Sri, is a big deal in the country of his birth and is the second-most senior federal title which can be bestowed on a Malaysian citizen. But to many football fans he is the embodiment of all that is wrong with the modern game, a successful businessman maybe, but one who understands little of the traditions and culture of football.

The boardroom fell silent. Simon Lim, the chief executive, hurriedly got up and moved to another seat as Tan Sri took his place next to the chairman. The great man gestured for water with a wave of his hand and the young PR man who had been taking minutes at the end of the table duly obliged. Tan was wearing a green suede bomber jacket over a smart grey polo shirt. It was in stark contrast to Mehmet Dalman's sober pinstripe suit and woven silk tie. Whatever their dress though, both men oozed wealth and confidence.

"Hello, Tim," said Tan breaking the reverential silence. "We met in Parliament at the end of season reception last year. See, I remember!" He chuckled and I think he may have winked.

It was meant to make me feel important. That he had remembered me. He was doing what I presumed he did every day. Displaying the reach of his wealth, influence, and unquestioned power. And I am embarrassed to say that a small spark of involuntary pride ran through my body that I had been singled out before my peers. Tan and I had a link, however tenuous and the other supporters in the room did not. He was playing a game, drawing me into his orbit and without knowing it I'd been snared.

The floor, or rather the boardroom table, was now Tan's. There had been an almighty row over this very table when the club left the crumbling Ninian Park ground in 2011 and crossed the road to its new home, the purpose-built steel and glass Cardiff City Stadium. The boardroom table was old, heavy and just didn't fit in with the new fixtures, indeed, the new image of football. Yet player contracts had been signed over this dark oak wood for a hundred years or more. The inlaid green leather had witnessed the signatures of Fred Keenor, the FA Cup winning hero of 1927 and the striker John Toshack in the Sixties. Sherwood, Stitfall, Bellamy and Legg would all have wriggled as they posed awkwardly for the press, sat between its arched legs pen poised over their new contract. The table had survived the transition from Ninian Park to the new boardroom. And now it too was all his. Tan's.

"I'm sure Tan Sri will answer any questions you have," said Mehmet generously. During our meeting he himself had been more than honest in his replies to our questions.

"I know this is a big deal for the fans," he'd told us almost embarrassed. "But I can't give you any empirical analysis of the need to rebrand the club and change from blue to red. At the end of the day it was Vincent's decision. Look, don't overestimate what a board or I as chairman can do when you have a single main shareholder."

I doubted Dalman would repeat those words now.

"Hang on, hang on, Mehmet," said Tan, "let me just say one thing," and he started on a rambling speech about the need for us all to 'modernise', put our differences aside and support the team. Yep, the same team that he had supported for all of four years.

Tan's reign at Cardiff City had been a rollercoaster ride. Before him there was no money to pay off debts and the Revenue were knocking at the door. The next thing we knew we were awash with cash for new signings, some of which proved to be very expensive disasters. Tan broached no criticism and had been dubbed a latter-day Bond villain by some in the media, sitting in the director's box wearing dark glasses, ostentatiously peeling on a pair of thin, black, leather gloves. He had been mocked for the way he wore the club's new, red replica top over his shirt and tie like a jumper, tucking it into his high-waisted trousers. Some said he looked like the school nerd.

But there was no question who was in control here. He launched into an attack on the profligacy of the previous manager who he had unceremoniously and publicly sacked. Dalman touched Tan's forearm to try to save him from himself.

"Let's have a couple of questions now, eh, Vincent?" But Tan Sri was having none of it and ploughed on with his views about the team, the ungrateful supporters and the limitless possibilities of the Chinese market, all of which of course preferred his lucky red to our stubborn and old-fashioned blue.

My attention wavered. I'd heard it all before. I looked up and saw two ancient thick cotton football shirts with laces in their necks neatly framed on the wall behind Mr Tan. One was blue. One was red. Cardiff versus Arsenal, the FA Cup final, 1927. Our most glorious day. Tradition.

"If you want a change, then get a new owner," Tan rumbled

on. I'd heard that one before as well. "Now get behind the red and support the team on Saturday." He'd finished with a flurry. Our time was up without a single question, and that was that.

It was a surreal experience, unnerving almost, as if every one of us present was part of an orchestrated charade. This was the world according to Vincent Tan and it was clear that it had been some time since he had been questioned, let alone challenged. None of us had any influence over this dollar billionaire and in his mind our silence meant acquiescence. Even if it did not, it made no difference.

As we stood up to leave Tan again took my hand. I smiled weakly and thanked him for his time. With his other, free hand Mr Tan tugged at his belt pulling his trousers firmly up over his polo shirt, just as he did with that replica red shirt on match days. It was a strange, nervous, defensive gesture and I wondered if it hinted at a tiny chink in his self-confidence. Then he said, "See, Tim. I told you we'd all get along just fine." He threw me another smile, and with that he was gone.

Change did come. Abruptly, out of the blue you might say, but again it was all orchestrated. Be careful what you wish for.

The world and his wife seemed to have been invited to the 'consultation' meeting at the Cardiff City Stadium. Fans, sponsors, journalists, councillors, bloggers and even two MPs who entered the room late having been given a private briefing by the club. The Malaysians are keen on making sure everything is squared off politically.

Was this it? After three years of division and derision had the club and its owner finally seen sense and decided to change the playing colours of the Bluebirds back to blue? The small talk in the packed room was nervous and overly polite. We were like small town officials gathering in anticipation of a royal visit, or a wedding party being kept waiting for the bride. Fake smiles all round and no-one wanting to say "For Pete's sake, can we just get on with it?" The walls showed blown-up pictures of the City's better days. Young men in their prime smiled at the camera. Most of them had by now left Cardiff and had moved on, some to better things, most to clubs in lower divisions.

I'd refused my reserved seat in the front row and was standing halfway up the aisle between the two sets of chairs chatting to Mr N-. He's a thick-set business bigwig and the only one who was happy to be overheard talking about the damage the club was doing to the city's international reputation. Mr N- had money, he was right and he didn't care what they thought of him. He was going to speak his mind. There was an interesting parallel with someone here but I decided not to dwell on it.

The murmuring dropped a notch and someone tapped my shoulder. I turned round to face the wedding party on its way to the high altar. Mehmet Dalman and his entourage had arrived. He was again in confident mood. Maybe he's like this every day but I wouldn't have wanted to have been in his shoes. This meeting was a gamble but then again he'd probably loaded the dice.

"Just keep a lid on things," he whispered conspiratorially in my ear. "If we play this right and show Vincent some respect we'll get what we want."

Sir. Yessir.

Mehmet took his party to the top table, introduced the team and invited us one by one to have our say. It was another charade but I knew my place. Vince talked about a hundred years of tradition. Mr N- spoke of the business opportunities lost. I talked about the importance of community. The councillors and MPs, only two of whom I actually recognised, spoke a lot and said nothing. The point was that they had spoken, their duty done and presence duly noted by the press.

We all thanked 'Mr Tan' for his investment – I couldn't bring myself to say Tan Sri as some of the more eager to please did – politely let off a little steam and stated our case yet again. The new chief executive, Ken Choo, thanked us for the respectful way we had outlined our case, told us to keep the faith and allow Vincent to make any decision in his own good time. Of course the decision had already been made and we knew it. We were all engaged in some sort of oriental protocol which we didn't quite understand but we did know that if we went along with it all it would serve us well. Did it go like this perhaps? You ask the Big Man for something. He thinks. Big Man refuses. You ask again. He refuses. You protest. He stands his ground. You change your tune, express gratitude and ask politely again. Big Man relents. Honourable resolution. I'm not sure if that's how it does go but it was beginning to feel that way.

The next day the inner circle of fans, of which I am ashamed to be a part, was summoned to the manager's office at the club's swish Vale of Glamorgan training centre ten miles west of the city. Russell Slade, the manager himself, was standing behind his desk in a tracksuit. He'd just finished training and would normally be the centre of attention the day before another 'must win' game.

"Will Whittingham and Gunnarsson start together again? Is Marshall over the injury? Do you think the formation works?" But not today.

Slade stood opposite his desk with his back to the whiteboard. It had a football pitch marked indelibly on it and a set of blue and red magnetic counters which they use to plan match tactics. He looked completely out of place in this hurried crisis meeting of directors and supporters. Mehmet was pleased to tell us what we all knew.

"Vincent was glad that you showed him respect. He's listened and has acceded." It was a very strange word to use. "We are returning to blue. The new Bluebird badge has a small Malaysian dragon on it of course. That's non-negotiable."

In fact the crest was already being designed but tomorrow, TOMORROW, we would play in blue at home for the first time in almost three years.

**

There were smiles all round at the press conference later that day. We'd won. It had been a hard, and at times an unpleasant, fight. But the supporters had been listened to and we, had, won. Mehmet lapped up the thanks and posed for pictures with the fans in their blue shirts. To be fair to the club they had petitioned the Football League and had been given permission for Cardiff to change their playing strip during the middle of the season. The players would be wearing blue shirts for the following day's game at home against Fulham.

As the camera shutters clicked Ken Choo, sporting a blue tie to make the point, read a statement from Vincent Tan. It said that he had come to his decision with "the guidance, blessing and influence" of his mother. "My wish is to unite and to make the club successful." Choo read slowly and deliberately so as not to risk any press misquote of Tan Sri.

"My mother, Madam Low Siew Beng, a devout Buddhist, who attended Cardiff City Football Club to watch them play, spoke to me on the importance of togetherness, unity and happiness."

So, it wasn't us after all. It was Vincent's mum who had won the day.

Even now, as we celebrated victory, Tan was making it clear that the colour we play in and the crest we wear were, and would always be, his choice. God bless Madam Low Siew Beng, but read between the lines and the statement we had waited so long to hear underlined, indeed magnified, the whole rotten set-up of football ownership in this country.

***

None of this mattered on the streets of Canton that night. There were drinks all round and by half-nine there were little jigs of happiness outside the Wetherspoon's. Every fan who had kept the faith, as well as many of those who had not, patted themselves and each other on the back. We had signed petitions, we'd made and sold thousands of our own blue shirts, chanted and waved our scarves. We'd pleaded, argued and protested. And we had won. I wanted to shout from the rooftops to the doubters and the kowtowers, "I told you so!" but I kept my silence and thanked anyone and everyone for the team effort. Magnanimity in victory is easy. There was however, one message I really wanted to hear. One person whose congratulations would have meant more to me than anyone, but nothing came from Chester.

His words that night in February 2013 still hurt. "This club is dead to me."

The press put it down to the blue shirts but we actually beat Fulham the next day. One-nil in an otherwise mediocre game. It was our second highest attendance of the season. We sang and we laughed and we chanted, "The boys are back in blue!" We were at last united. As one. It was like the old days. Only it wasn't. Cardiff City were indeed back in blue but this wasn't my Cardiff City any more. My girlfriend had cheated on me. I'd forgiven her, chased her and she'd finally said OK. I'd taken her back into my arms and given her once again my unconditional love. We'd been together for more than twenty-five years and there could be no going back. Or could there? For the last three of those years she had shown that she was not really mine. In fact she had been in thrall to another master. Our relationship was not the same any more. How could it be? We had become a couple who stay together 'for the sake of the children', only in my case the child had made his own mind up. No, she was sullied, no longer wholly mine. There is part of our relationship that can never be fixed. And that I will never forgive.

Kicking off
in North Korea

April 2013

"WHERE YOU FROM?" It was a simple question from a smartly dressed young man paying his drinks bill in US dollars in the basement bar of the Yanggakdo Hotel. Chester and I froze for a moment unsure how to respond. This was our first uncontrolled conversation with a real North Korean. A real North Korean! We had been told that any such contact should not happen and since we'd arrived in Pyongyang our every move had been monitored.

Nothing is quite what it seems in the hermit state that is North Korea. As we drove through the outskirts of its model capital city, gangs of soldiers in rows of four marched across a building site. One man at the front carried an outsized national flag with its splendid red star on a long pole across the parched yellow earth. They marched in perfect quickstep like a wind-up model army. We could have been watching a Soviet propaganda film from the 1930s. Thankfully they were not digging trenches for war. "Most of the construction here is done by the military," our guide informed us. This was just another block of flats going up.

Chester was halfway through his gap year before university. I was chuffed that my boy still wanted to travel with his father rather than bungee jump in Cairns or drink himself stupid in Magaluf. Maybe it is the social realist architecture or the hammer and sickle symbols but we share a passion for post-communist societies. Over the years we'd been through Eastern Europe, Russia and Cuba. We arrived in Pyongyang fresh from Cambodia, Vietnam and China. This though, North Korea, was the real thing. "Actually existing communism" as they used to say. And the reality of this socialist dream was both sobering and enlightening.

Downtown Pyongyang is dreary and grey. Slab after slab of monolithic tower blocks stretch into the distance. The streets are wide. There are few cars on them but the buses and trams are jam-packed. Every few hundred yards a massive public building, monument or sculpture overlooks a square or peers down a long, wide set of ceremonial steps. The Triumphal Arch, "higher than the one in Paris", stands on the very spot where Kim Il-sung returned to the city in 1945 after his famous victory over the Japanese. The Korean Workers Party Foundation Monument is a real gem of brutal socialist architecture. Three muscular arms carved out of solid rock reach to the sky, holding a sickle, a hammer and a traditional drawing brush. They symbolise the coming together of farmer, worker and intellectual in the struggle for socialism. It was good to see the intellectuals getting in on the act of this particular revolution.

Our tour group was an eclectic mix of travellers, most of whom had 'done' the usual exotic or dangerous places.

"Come from Cambodia, have you?"

"Yeah, we did it the first year they let anyone in."

"Iran?"

"Sure, got in overland from Syria."

There was a gay couple from Germany and a guy who worked in the London Mayor's office who tried to hide in the group photos in case they were, as he put it, "someday used against me." And then there was Ron and his wife Margaret, a chatty couple from California. He'd been in business and she had been an air hostess. Ron had one of those large cameras which should be too big to be digital, like a sports photographer by the side of the pitch or a paparazzo waiting to pounce outside a nightclub, and he pointed it everywhere.

In the Yanggakdo bar, the night we'd made first contact with a real North Korean, we'd also met Juan from Barcelona. He had paid through the nose for a one-to-one tour of the country but we seemed to meet him at every place we stopped. Juan had spent the last twenty years trying to visit every country in the world.

"All 193 members of the United Nations," he told us proudly.

"How long do you stay in each place?" I asked bitchily after my third beer.

"Look," he said. "I am not a stamp collector. I wanna see these places."

We actually got on well and I could see Chester's eyes light up as he pondered spending the rest of his life following in the footsteps of Juan.

"The worst of it?" he said, "Those South Sea Islands. You get one flight delayed, the whole trip goes belly up."

There was an unspoken smugness about us all. We quietly knew that getting into and out of North Korea would top anyone else's travelling story. We tried to converse with the Korean at the bar but his English was a bit rough.

"Beautiful country you have," said Chester, tending, as one does with locals abroad to overdo the praise.

First contact. Good. Nice and bland. Let's see where this goes.

"Yes, we are here for a week. Looking forward to seeing the city and the countryside."

I looked at Chester and then at our new friend. Would he be in trouble for talking to us? Would we be in trouble for talking to him? He mumbled something about friendship but went back to the pool table and his friends. I think they had all been drinking heavily.

We'd had a long day. Mrs L- had us up early for the city tour. The scale of everything in Pyongyang is impressive. Two massive bronze statues of Kim Il-sung and his son and successor Kim Jong-il point knowingly down the landscaped gardens and across the Taedong River at the Party Monument beyond. The original statues were coated in gold but the United Nations took exception to this extravagance, threatened to stop its aid, and the gold leaf was stripped off. This is a place of reverence and we'd joined the thousands of soldiers, schoolchildren and factory workers on Kim Il-sung's 101st birthday to lay flowers before the two giant leaders. We were ordered into lines and told how to bow to pay our respects.

Images of both men peer down from every public building. Their smiling faces adorn the walls of every office. There are even portraits of them in the carriages of the Pyongyang metro. When I peered into the dimly lit flats I could see the two identikit pictures of them on the wall. No family snaps, just the official images of the Great Leader and the Dear Leader. Most people in the city wore badges bearing their faces on their left breast.

Below the monumental sculptures and public buildings of course are the people themselves. Small and insignificant against these giants, they rarely looked at us in our garish T-shirts and jeans. The people of Pyongyang dress smartly, the men in suits, the women in somewhat dowdy colours, but their faces betrayed no emotion. We were allowed to ride on the metro, well, for three stops anyway. It was immaculately clean and where you would normally have advertisements on the walls of the stations there were intricate mosaics showing idyllic scenes of farming, industry and scientific progress. We were ushered into the train and all sat quietly in one carriage. A group of three Koreans stepped in too but as they saw these strange Western faces in front of them they stopped in their tracks. No-one spoke and as if on cue they turned around and found another presumably untainted car.

Despite asking Mrs L- more than once, we did not visit a roadside bar or café. Chester and I knew that is where the heart of a nation lies, people hanging out talking and drinking. Society. We'd discussed politics with the locals in smoke-filled bars in Armenia, swapped addresses in a café in Belarus and talked Hoxha and football in equal measure in Albania. But not here. All that human texture and colour that is the very stuff of travelling was missing. The basement bar of the Yanggakdo and its nervous clientele was as close as we got.

The shops downtown had no window displays, no advertising. The only colour came from large red slogans picked out in traditional script across the front of buildings and on lamp-posts. When we did leave the city the hillsides sported Hollywood-style signs in giant lettering. They forewarned of death to the Americans and praised the unfaltering commitment of the Kims to build socialism and reunify the Korean people.

Street posters showed the twisted face of a soldier urging the people to resist. Another showed three smiling women singing into microphones. Behind them, the shadow of the rocket which had launched the Korean satellite into space that February. Its mission was peaceful, said the Koreans. The Americans took a different view and the United Nations promptly tightened economic sanctions on this already poor nation and its twenty-three million people. It was this move which had led to North Korea saying it could no longer guarantee our safety there. On the ground however, it just didn't feel that way. Life went on as normal. Well, as normal as it can in this kaleidoscopic society. Even on our visit to the demilitarised zone along the long closed main road to Seoul, the capital of the South, we saw no sign of a military build-up. Yet state television seemed to be whipping the people up into a frenzy. Children's cartoons were followed by images of warfare. Fearsome artillery rockets lit up the troops' faces as they raced across the night-time battlefield. Then came a crude animation of the White House burning after a successful missile strike. The commentary bordered on the hysterical. Even at the circus the trapeze artists swung below a revolving model of the dreaded missile.

The anti-American rhetoric finally got to Ron. On the bus

that morning Mrs L- had just given another account of the atrocities inflicted by the Yanks on the peace-loving Koreans over the last fifty years. Up stood Ron. "For crying out loud. I'm a socialist and I've come here to see what's happening to your country. Give us a break, would you." There were embarrassed smiles from the rest of us. Chester guffawed. Mrs L- acted like nothing had happened and carried on.

Pyongyang looked and felt like a twenty-four-hour theme park based on what American film-makers thought a Russian city looked like in the 1950s. The whole nation appeared to be in the grip of a cult. The cult of personality of the Kims. The Great Leader's grandson, Kim Jong-un is now the Supreme Commander and leader of the Workers Party. I turned to one of our guides for some explanation.

"Why do you venerate them so much?"

Mrs L- tilted her head and smiled at me. "Are you in any way religious?" she said. When I said no, she shrugged. "Then you probably won't understand us."

How much of the hype the people actually believe is hard to judge. There is no internet, no outside television or independent newspaper. All communication is strictly controlled. North Koreans only get one narrow world view. Three generations have now been fed a diet of anti-imperialist propaganda and the country has been on a war footing since 1945. The Korean peninsula has long been the battleground for major powers and ideologies. The Japanese, Chinese, Russians and the Americans all have pretty shameful histories here. The Koreans' anger is understandable. Power politics continues to be played out here in the final act of the Cold War. Everyone we spoke to honestly believed an attack by the Americans was imminent.

Back in the basement bar of the Yanggakdo Hotel our friend came back to the bar and drained his drink. "British, eh?" We nodded, unsure where this was going. He paused. "Britain, America. You are as one," he said with a flourish of his hand. "When war comes. You no friends of Korea." We smiled nervously until another man who had been half-listening to us stepped closer and tapped our new friend on his shoulder with a packet of American cigarettes. The gesture clearly said 'time to go!'

***

I was converted to football in the late 1980s. At school it was rugby all the way. Well, it was the 1970s, I was a teenager, Wales were world-beaters and rugby fitted the macho culture of the time. But when I returned to Cardiff a decade later and was taken once again to the faded glory of Ninian Park, I was hooked. Football consumed me and I soon began to see it as an important viewfinder for society as a whole. Terrace culture encompasses clothes and music but it offers more than a simple shared interest. It enthuses and engages people so that we live parallel lives through our love of football. The film director Johnny Owen described himself as "walking to a different beat" as a football fan in the south Wales valleys when most of his mates were rugby boys. I have managed to strike up conversations across the world solely through a shared knowledge of some obvious and sometimes totally obscure facts about football. I knew that Chester and I would have to watch a match in North Korea.

We badgered Mrs L- from day one. "It would be really good to watch a football match while we are here. It's what we do in our country and I am sure the people of Korea all enjoy football just like we do." I was trying to appeal to her national vanity: Listen lady! Here's an opportunity to show us the fatherland as a normal country. Show us a game and we'll go home and say you're normal, that you like the footie, just like the rest of us. But of course Mrs L- was working to a script set down by the Party. There was nothing in it for her to deviate from the pre-arranged, stage managed visits. Innovation? Spontaneity? What was I thinking of? But amazingly, after two days, and after we had gathered a good dozen or so fellow travellers to our cause, she announced that we could indeed attend a match. Result.

You'll not hear Sky Sport's Jeff Stelling saying, "There'll be dancing on the streets of Pyongyang," anytime soon. Or anyone else for that matter. Because the North Koreans take their footie as seriously as their politics. That is to say, very seriously. This was the pariah country's match of the day – Pyongyang, the capital, versus Amrokkang, the crack army outfit.

The game was a sell-out though you'd never have guessed it. As we entered the 50,000 seater Kim Il-sung Stadium below the watchful eyes of the Eternal President and Great Leader, not forgetting his son Kim Jong-il, there was no-one to be seen. There were no queues, no turnstiles and certainly no hot dog stands or programme sellers.

Once inside it was a different matter. Every seat was taken and row upon row of men sat silently, wearing identical dark suits and red ties, every one of them sporting a tiny enamel badge on their left breast. No, not the crest of Pyongyang FC, but of the Great Leader himself.

The artificial pitch looked immaculate under the spring morning sun. Kick-off was at half past nine, but then it was a bank holiday. The match and the bank holiday were to mark the 101st birthday of Kim Il-sung but it was a strange sort of celebration. Maybe it was the early start but there were no chants and no flags or scarves to be seen, just a quiet murmur around the stands, as if in anticipation. Some sections were reserved for soldiers who were all turned out in identical olive-green uniforms and broad-brimmed hats. I don't know if they were under orders to attend but some were quietly reading paperbacks and showed no interest in the game.

Amrokkang looked stronger in the first half though it was a scrappy match. The 3G pitch and a ball which seemed to bounce and sway at the slightest touch didn't help. Pyongyang fought back and won a penalty, though you would be hard pressed to know that from the reaction of the crowd. There was none. Chester, who knows a thing or two about the beautiful game, turned to me. "It's not football though, Dad, is it? Really." So we decided to inject some old-style British terrace atmosphere of our own and chanted,

"One-nil to the referee, one-nil to the referee."

The dozen or so Westerners who had joined us in the VIP box (at thirty euros a seat – hard currency only please) laughed at us. They got the joke. Juan and the Germans joined in. That just made us bolder.

"Pyongyang ooh ooh! Pyongyang ooh ooh!"

But the locals just stared at us. I wondered if we had caused offence but no-one asked us to stop. We were just ignored. In a land where it seemed you must ask permission to speak, this show of individuality, of spontaneity, was not seen as rude, threatening or aggressive. They stared blankly at us. I think they thought we were just, well, a little odd.

Our every movement in North Korea had been strictly controlled. Two women guides led us from the front while the mysterious Mr M- who hardly spoke, brought up the back of our tour group. Was he minding us or making sure our guides kept to the script that all was rosy in this socialist utopia? We had only just made it in. The day before we arrived, the present leader Kim Jung-un had threatened a nuclear attack on America. One of the borders with China was closed and we'd been checking the UK government's travel advice as best we could from Beijing. BBC World news would later report this game as an attempt by the country's leaders to show that it was 'business as usual' during these dangerous times. Me, I just wanted to watch some football.

"So football is big here in Korea is it, Mr M-?" I thought this would be the perfect icebreaker.

"Yes. All men love it," he said without breaking a smile. Success, I thought. He speaks.

Apparently there are three leagues in North Korean football but because they all play at different times of the year and because of the country's history of underhand international player transfers, these clubs cannot play in south Asian tournaments. Mind you, I cannot think of a single North Korean playing outside his country, dodgy transfer deal or otherwise.

The national side uses the official name of the country, the Democratic People's Republic of Korea. They won't use 'North' because they say they are one country even though they have been technically at war with the South since the end of the civil war in 1953. Their greatest footballing moment came in the 1966 World Cup when they beat Italy 2–0 to reach the quarter-finals. They also qualified for the 2010 finals in South Africa. During that tournament North Korea's coach, Kim Jong-hun, told the media that he received "regular tactical advice during matches" from Kim Jong-il "using mobile phones that are not visible to the naked eye" and purportedly developed by the Dear Leader himself. Of course. The national team was struggling when we were there and had not qualified for the following year's World Cup in Brazil. Their last game was a goalless draw in a friendly against Cuba.

Back on the pitch at the Kim Il-sung Stadium, Amrokkang had got one back. Another penalty. Why the referee had to confer with the linesman I don't know. The Pyongyang striker was taken down five yards inside the box. In fact the ref was having a nightmare of a game though you would not have known that from the reaction of the players and officials. The technical areas on the side of the pitch where coaching staff usually harangue the referee, the opposition and their own players were empty all game. Neither manager ventured out of the dugout nor was there any high-fiving or pats on the back when players were substituted. Now I like to watch controlled football, but not quite like this.

Amazingly I'd read that there was a riot at a football match here in 2005 in that same Kim Il-sung Stadium which was a sea of tranquillity for our visit. Soldiers and police had to step in as violence erupted when North Korea lost a World Cup qualifying match to Iran. Bottles, stones and chairs were thrown onto the pitch when a Korean player was sent off. The unrest continued after the final whistle, and match officials were unable to leave the pitch for more than twenty minutes. Thousands of angry fans surrounded the stadium preventing the Iranian players from getting on their bus. It reportedly took two hours to disperse the crowd.

"The atmosphere on the pitch and outside the pitch was not a sports atmosphere," Iran's coach Branko Ivanković said rather understatedly. "It's very disappointing when you feel your life is not safe. My players tried to get to the bus after the game but it was not possible – it was a very dangerous situation."

Andrei Lankov, a North Korea academic based in the South, wrote, "If I were Kim Jong-il, I would be quite terrified. If people can riot about football, then they can as well about the food distribution or somebody's arrest. Something like this would have been unthinkable in Pyongyang ten years ago." As it would be today, but Kim Jong-un is still in power and the likelihood of the regime collapsing of its own accord seems as far away as ever.

Surprise surprise there was some half-time entertainment for us. A brass band piped up behind the goal. But immediately and as if they'd been waiting for their cue, another band behind the opposite goal struck up. They were playing different tunes. Were they bands from different sections of the armed forces competing against each other? Who knows?

The match went into stoppage time as the fourth official held up a board showing two minutes. Pyongyang were pressing hard. "Surely it's all over now?" said Chester, who was the only one still watching the game as if any of it mattered. The clock showed they had played for ninety-four minutes. At last the crowd seemed to rouse themselves, if only a little, at the prospect of a goal. I looked at my watch but the referee didn't look at his. Finally, Pyongyang scored with a low shot following some good interpassing. It was the very last kick of the oddest game I have ever watched. Maybe the referee was under orders to ensure a home win on this special public holiday. Either way I would like to think the crowd went home happy. But with no emotion one way or the other on the faces of the soldiers and party faithful as they marched silently out of the Kim Il-sung Stadium, I simply couldn't tell. "Pyongyang ooh ooh! Pyongyang ooh ooh!"

***

The border between North and South Korea is said to be the most heavily militarised in the world. I don't know what that means really as it's supposed to be the 'Demilitarised Zone', the DMZ. It's 160 miles long and if it is the most dangerous border around then it's a really good advertisement for deterrence. A visit there is de rigueur for most visitors to either side and as this was to allegedly be the front line in any missile inspired spat who were we to argue? But first, lunch.

"What kind of dog is this?" asked the civil servant from London. The vegetarians in our party looked aghast. After a slight conflab with the waiter, Mrs L- said, "Sorry, but they don't know." Three of us had taken the plunge and ordered dog at the upmarket hotel in the city of Kaesong, some eight kilometres from the border with the South. I will try anything once. The trouble was, this dog was served in a soup.

Panmunjom was where the armistice which brought to an end the Korean War was signed. That was in 1953 but, as we had been repeatedly told, this was not a 'real' peace treaty and the previous week the People's Democratic Republic of Korea had declared it was again on a war footing with the South. The war of words between the two ideological claimants to the Korean peninsula had started up again. North and South, the East and the West were all having their say in a rerun of Cold War rhetoric.

Before entering the Demilitarised Zone we were herded into a purpose built shelter, and given a lengthy lecture by a military commander on how the South had started the war by invading the North in 1950. This version of events is of course hotly disputed by the South. Only after our history lesson were we driven to the border itself.

"Look!" shouted the German teacher who until then had been the quietest member of our group. "You can see the South's flag," he said excitedly. In the hazy distance you could make out a long pole swaying with the blue and red disc of South Korea.

"OK. You can take a picture, but do it quickly," said Mrs L-.

Ron was positively jumping. We had all become slightly jittery on the road south. We had seen no evidence of a full-scale military build-up despite both countries, North and South, saying they were ready for a war. More words. Dangerous words.

But as we got out of the bus at the border we had heard gunfire nearby. We 'Westerners' looked at each other alarmed. "No worry," said Mrs L- rather too briskly, "they are doing building work in the next field. No worry." She was trying to reassure us though there was no way she could have known where the noise was coming from. It was probably some sort of practice drill for the soldiers serving their time in this seemingly tranquil but oh-so-significant stretch of farmland. More than a hundred families live in the DMZ, planting rice and raising cattle on flat fields between the barbed wire, tank traps and checkpoints. To whom they would really like to owe their allegiance is anyone's guess.

North Korea is said to have more than a million men and women under arms. It's difficult to know how well equipped or trained they are. One of our other minders, Ms P-, a proud member of the Workers' Party, had done three years' military service. She was tiny but always immaculately turned out in a sharply pressed black suit with the ubiquitous image of Kim Il-sung, the Great Leader, on a badge on her chest. "Of course I was a teacher when I was in the Army," she said. Hardly the front line.

Mrs L-, though, had let slip that she'd lived in the West. "My father worked for the International Atomic Energy Authority. We lived in Geneva for many years," she said. Chester thought we were on to something.

"So she must know that all this is a fantasy? I mean, to have lived in Switzerland and then not to have seen things here as we see them. Perhaps they have a hold on her. On all of them. You know, 'You're the lucky ones. You get to travel. But you can forget all that if you put one foot out of place. Understand?'"

Mrs L- was certainly pure of *Juche* thought. She wouldn't let any discussion on politics or the central place of their leaders to every facet of life go very far, closing it down with, "It's difficult to explain" or, "We must move on now". It was not a convincing performance. I'd read that everyone who lives in Pyongyang is privileged, just like Mrs L- and her family. Nice apartment, plenty of food and entertainment, even the odd visit to China with your colleagues if you were really lucky. But if you don't toe the line, it's back to the hills and abject poverty. You and your extended family.

Juche is the official political ideology of North Korea. It can be loosely translated as 'self-reliance' or 'independence' and is Kim Il-sung's own variant of Marxism-Leninism, his "original, brilliant and revolutionary contribution to national and international thought". *Juche* teaches that the Korean people are masters of their own destiny. It emphasises the individual, the nation state and its sovereignty. Its principles include moving the nation towards *chaju* (independence, especially from the Soviet Union and China) through the construction of *charip* (the national economy) and an emphasis upon *chawi* (self-defence) in order to establish socialism. Maybe, but it has also led to authoritarianism, isolation, ethnic nationalism and the cult of personality.

The border itself has two squat buildings facing each other over a low line of concrete. That thin grey line actually goes through the four single-storey blue huts which until very recently were used for negotiations between the two enemies. All that stopped after the February missile launch and the UN sanctions. Set back from these now empty huts are the two main buildings, visitors' centres I suppose you would call them, both bristling with antennae and cameras. Each side watching the other. Watching and waiting.

Steps take you down to the borderline itself but with South Korean soldiers now just yards away we kept our distance. Both sets of guards were facing us, young men wearing round helmets and fearsome stares. As our party chatted and took pictures three American marines came into view from behind the central hut. They towered above the shorter southern Korean regulars. In their combat gear, their bulging shoulders and thigh pockets packed with goodness know what, they swaggered towards the grey concrete line, stopped there with their hands on their hips and eyeballed us. They stood firm and paused slightly too long for comfort, before taking a couple of orchestrated steps backwards. No wonder the northern soldiers look the other way. The official reason given is that they are looking north to protect the compatriots, not south to antagonise the Americans. Whatever the truth we were glad to get back on the bus. It had been a fascinating but unnerving experience.

It would be easy to dismiss all this posturing as a game of toy soldiers. But history, flags and ideology make for a potent mix and it is unlikely this checkpoint will be stamping anybody's passport soon. America and China, who are still playing a power game by proxy on this sad peninsula, are in no hurry to see the unification of Korea. The North is impoverished and the economy underdeveloped, in stark contrast to the booming capitalist South. The last thing South Korea or China wants is twenty-three million refugees, most of them poor farmers, hurrying across the border. And so the posturing, the waiting and the watching goes on.

In the Kaesong hotel, Chester had turned from his vegetarian banquet and gestured with his knife to my steaming soup. "You know what it smells like, don't you?" I didn't answer. I raised another piece of the fatty, glutinous strips from the bowl. He was right of course. It smelt of wet dog. It was another new Korean experience for me. But just like the sad border with its fear and loathing, not one I am in a hurry to try again.

All quiet
on the eastern front

June 2013

MY NEW FRIEND Bruno wasn't a football hooligan. But then how was I to tell? The captain of the Croatian supporters' team was certainly a good singer as he led his compatriots, right arm across his chest, clenched fist on heart, in a rousing nationalistic song. It may even have been the Croatian national anthem. His team's vocal efforts resounded off the arched brick ceiling of the Kryivka cellar bar beneath Lviv's historic Rynok central square. Kryivka means 'bunker' or 'hiding place' in Ukrainian and this is where the partisan nationalist Ukrainians were said to have held out during the war. The blood vessels on the young men's necks bulged at the effort in the midsummer heat. Welcome to Eurofan 2013 where friendships are made through football, and the odd drink or five.

Lvov, or Lviv as it is called in Ukrainian, is the self-appointed cultural capital of western Ukraine. With its cobbled streets, fine universities and graceful yellow Habsburg buildings you feel you are on a film set, rather like Prague before the tourists arrived. Lviv was left unscathed despite being occupied by both the Soviets and the Germans during the Second World War and is now a UNESCO World Heritage site. It is also home to Eurofan, a supporters' tournament that attracts teams from across Europe to celebrate friendship through football.

For the footballing authorities in Ukraine, Eurofan is an opportunity to shake off some grim images of the game out east in a country desperate to display its European credentials. EU membership is the nation's long-term goal and this is a small way of saying, "We're one of you. We're looking west." Cultural diplomacy, I suppose. For us supporters it is a chance to play and socialise with other fans in a different, beautiful and slightly exotic city. The results, on or off the pitch, frankly, take a back seat.

British teams have done pretty well in Lviv in recent years. The Glasgow Rangers Supporters' team won the tournament in 2009. Liverpool too have played here. My team, Wales Supporters, once reached the quarter-finals. OK, we didn't win the group to get there but went through after the Polish team from Kraków was arrested en masse following the stabbing of a doorman in the rather tacky but ever popular Millennium nightclub. The Eurofan website notes that the Poles didn't make it through to the next round due to "technical reasons".

As can happen in football we supporters perhaps turn a blind eye to the excesses of the game, be that the crazy pay structure in the Premiership, foul language on the terraces or the now thankfully isolated incidents of hooliganism. But racism? In the modern game and in a friendly tournament? Surely not.

Oleg Soldatenko supports the local Ukrainian club Karpaty Lviv and is one of the volunteers who set up Eurofan. "Sure, we've had our fair share of problems with hooligans. My club's no exception," he told me. "Part of the reason we set up Eurofan was to show the world that Ukraine and Poland could run the European Championship without it all kicking off." And he was right. Euro 2012 was, for the most part, violence free. But both host countries have in the past shown the all-too-ugly side of the beautiful game.

Clubs across southern and central Europe are still blighted by hooligans. Some are just madly passionate about their team. Others, however, adopt fascist politics, are openly racist and homophobic, and arrange fights with other gangs before and sometimes during games.

Oleg and his team of volunteers are trying to change perceptions and they are keen to show a more constructive side to football. During the Eurofan tournament supporters visit children's homes and charities with gifts of sports kit, toiletries and sweets. John O'Neill, the captain of the Republic of Ireland team, told me how his players had raised more than six hundred euros. "The lads really got into it and this is our chance to give something back to this city. The craic is great here and everyone is so welcoming," he said.

Eurofan may badge itself as the friendly football festival, but the dark side of soccer in Eastern Europe can all too readily raise its head. During Eurofan 2009 I had seen three black players barred from returning to an enclosed training pitch to collect their shin pads. "You are not welcome here," said a Polish skinhead in broken English and made a gesture as if slitting his throat. Ironically, the Poles were targeting the Serbia supporters' team, a group of fans known only too well in Britain for racially abusing players at international fixtures.

That same year the Wales Supporters' team had played a bruising encounter against the Ukrainians but all was forgotten as the teams left the field. The Ukrainian midfielder who had tormented the Welsh defence struggled to pull off his drenched yellow and blue jersey. He had the words 'White Hooligan' in old Germanic script tattooed across his belly. And on the back of his neck was a blue cross and a circle, the symbol of white power. He was big and he looked mean, but on that all-white pitch he was remarkably friendly and as we walked off we happily discussed all things football, and the price of the local beer.

It was intriguing then to see the German team FC Schalke 04 literally flying an anti-fascist flag at the tournament. These supporters pride themselves on their political correctness and boast the largest anti-fascist fan club in Germany. Their avowed aim is to be "the coolest Nazi-free zone in the world". Schalke's tournament shirt for Lviv showed a boot kicking a football which enclosed a swastika. Yes, I thought. I want one of those.

At the Eurofan closing ceremony at the crumbling SKA Stadium, I asked Schalke's female manager if we could meet up later to follow the time honoured tradition and exchange shirts. She said that she'd like to but that maybe it would be a bit awkward. She was visibly shaken. "They've stolen our flag and warned us not to go into town tonight or we'll get it," she told me. I didn't ask her who "they" were. Could it be the lads from St Petersburg who had announced their arrival at the tournament with a thick, black smoke bomb as they raised a skull and crossbones flag above the terrace? Was it my new friends, the tuneful Croats? The Czechs even?

I offered some mealy-mouthed words about sticking together to the woman from Schalke, as I had done to the black Serbs, but none of us reported any of these incidents to Oleg and the organising team. Our Ukrainian guides, language students at the prestigious University of Lviv, offered their sympathies too but basically shrugged their shoulders as if to say, "That's just the way it is".

The year after the Euro 2012 finals things seemed to have calmed down. There was no trouble in Lviv and Eurofan lived up to its slogan, "Football, Fun, Friendship". At the same caged pitch where I had witnessed naked racism, the red hand of Ulster, Northern Ireland's flag, flew alongside the Republic's tricolour while the home-made banners of the Bulgarian and Zenit St Petersburg teams were tied to the fencing behind the other goal. It was a colourful celebration of everyone's shared passion for football. All the players were there to win but when a team's numbers were depleted through injury or too much of the local Lvivske beer, players from different nations stepped into the breach to make sure there was a full side. "Our team should be renamed the United Nations," said the Wales coach, Neil Dymock. "We had two Georgians, a Dane and a couple of Ukrainians play for us."

The day's football over, we took up the Swedish fans' invitation to a midsummer celebration. Players chatted in broken English and sang late into the night. The men from the Republic and Northern Ireland, Russia and Georgia, who on home ground would probably never speak to each other let alone share a drink, swapped shirts and email addresses, forgetting for this week at least, any differences their countries might have. The vodka flowed, the volume pumped up, then someone lit a flare and under the pink phosphorescent haze young men danced topless to a thumping Euro disco beat.

This year's final pitted the Bulgaria national team against Romania's Dinamo Bucharest. The game ended 1–1 and the dreaded penalty shoot-out ensued. Bulgaria ran out winners and celebrated wildly on the pitch. I watched the closing ceremony with Lydia Shaley, a polyglot law graduate who volunteers every summer as a guide to the visiting teams. "They're always a great bunch of lads. And I get to practise my Russian with the Eastern European teams and my English with the Welsh and the Irish," she said.

We stood on the shaky terrace and watched the victorious players parade around the pitch below us. One man's shirt caught my eye. He was in his late forties and about sixteen stone but had just about squeezed into his football jersey. I guessed he was the team manager. On the back in Cyrillic script was the word "ДУЧЕ" (Duce), a nod to Italian fascist leader Mussolini. Below that were printed the numbers 8 8. The eighth letter of the alphabet is H, and H H is code among fascists for 'Heil Hitler'. After a week of great football and friendship, it left a slightly bitter taste. Lydia looked embarrassed. "Things are improving over here, honest," she said, "but it's going to take a bit of time."

Back on the big stage of the professional game that year Holland played Poland in a warm-up match for the real European finals. Mark van Bommel, the Dutch national captain, said that during the game his black players had been subjected to monkey chants. The Dutch FA said the chanting was mixed with Polish fans making political statements but that they would make no official complaint. Officials, players, fans then, at one. Silence, as they say, is golden. Isn't it?

Firecrackers and flares

September 2013

BOSNIA AND HERZEGOVINA had qualified for the World Cup finals for the first time in the country's short history. The plane was booked, they were off to Brazil. The national team's success may have at last united a country of diverse peoples with Serbs, Croats and Bosniaks for once celebrating together. "Football's a way of bringing people together," said Bosnia's then Sports Minister, Salmir Kaplan. But in Bosnia-Herzegovina, old habits, like tribal loyalties, die hard.

We crossed the border from Croatia over a narrow bridge spanning the river Sava at Brod. Or Slavonski Brod depending on which side of the river you are. But hold on, this was not Bosnia. The bold blue sign welcomed us to Republika Srpska, an autonomous Serb entity within the complicated set-up that is modern-day Bosnia-Herzegovina. An independent country, yes, but still not united it seems.

The evidence of the war that had so deeply divided the former Yugoslavia was still painfully clear as we drove south-west along windy roads through lush farmland. For mile after mile, we saw no-one. Yes, there were homes in tiny hamlets of three or four houses either side of the road, but they all lay abandoned. Nobody was sitting on the veranda. There were no chickens scratching in the yard. No children playing in the overgrown grass. These once sturdy three-storey buildings lay in ruin, every window put out, the walls pockmarked with gunfire, others bearing the blackened imprint of scorch marks where families had been burned out of their homes.

Chester broke the silence in the car. "But these were normal people. Like us. They watched TV at night. Had a beer and a laugh. Where did the hatred come from? They were neighbours, for Chrissake." Just then a single newly-built house appeared, smart, clean and with a shiny new car sitting proudly on the drive. It was directly opposite another burned out house. The Republika Srpska flag blew from a skinny wavering pole in the well-kept garden. Why build a new home when there were perfectly good frames still standing? Were they ashamed of moving into the bedrooms of a family who had at best been forced across the river simply for being Croatian?

In the Sarajevo City Museum the stories of hatred, fear, loathing and suffering were piled one on top of the other. There were accusations of atrocities and excesses on both sides. The tangible history of this city hits you at every turn. Outside the now rebuilt Sacred Heart Cathedral is a splodge of red. Mortar rounds landing on concrete create a unique fragmentation pattern which looks like a floral arrangement. The locals filled the holes with red resin to mark where the mortar shells fell, killing whoever happened to be there, shopping, going to church, going to school. A mortar fired from a hill half a mile away doesn't discriminate. There are dozens of these red markers all over the city. They call them "Sarajevo roses". One by one they are disappearing as the asphalt is replaced. Memories fading little by little.

We were staying at the Markale hostel right next to the market where a shell landed in February 1994, killing sixty-eight people and injuring 144. The images of that massacre, body parts strewn on the pavement and the pictures in the museum of summary executions in the street and people running for their lives across Sarajevo's notorious sniper alley, seemed at odds with what is now a bustling capital city where different cultures appeared to co-exist. I was woken at 4.30 in the morning by the muezzin calling the faithful to prayer. Then at 7.30 the bells of the cathedral rang out to celebrate the first mass of the day. There was something reassuring about this age-old devotion, whichever God you worship. The city seemed calm and confident, cosmopolitan and tolerant. Maybe at last there was peace in Sarajevo. Perhaps they'd all just had enough of the hating.

The approach to the Otoka football ground took us past the mighty Istiklal džamija mosque. A gift from the Indonesian people, its two towering minarets guard the wide, black central dome. As the football fans in their red and white scarves straggled past the mosque, a wedding party spilled out through its heavy double doors. The young men were dressed in dark suits, some women wore a full niqāb, others simple headscarves. One woman stood out. She was wearing a very short, yellow mini skirt and tottered on her high heels as she came down the steps. The image seemed to be making an unintended statement: "There is no 'one' Muslim in Sarajevo. You want to cover your face? OK. You want to show off your legs. That's OK too." And as we waited for kick-off in the away stand, the Muslim call to prayer reverberated from the minarets across the pitch towards us.

This Saturday afternoon the capital's third team, Olimpik Sarajevo, was taking on local rivals and the runners-up of last year's Bosnian Premier League, FK Sarajevo. Both clubs were formed out of war. Olimpik in October 1993 during the siege of Sarajevo, while FK was set up in the nascent Yugoslavia just after the Second World War. Now football around here has a bit of history. During the Bosnian war both sides recruited street fighters from football clubs. The groups of supporters called themselves 'Ultras', the European shorthand for passionate fans, mostly loud and peaceful but sometimes violent too. FK Sarajevo's 'Hordes of Evil' Ultras joined the Bosnian government side as did the 'Maniacs' of Željezničar, FK's main rivals. But that was then wasn't it? History, as they say.

Two flares fizzed in the middle of the packed terrace spewing pink smoke over the crowd and across the pitch, obscuring the green playing surface. As one, the supporters started a low, guttural chant, and then they stopped. There was a second of cold silence before a sharp single drumbeat. The crack of the drum echoed back from the opposite terrace heralding another round of chanting. The fans were egged on by a man with a megaphone precariously hanging from a post at pitchside. The almost military precision of it was just a little unsettling.

We stood among the FK faithful who filled the larger side of this tiny stadium. Olimpik have very few fans and on today's evidence even fewer who would openly show their allegiance. The game was not much to write home about but despite the poor performances there was a fiery passion in the crowd. Every decision the referee made was contested. Firecrackers punctuated the singing and the game had to be stopped more than once as flares were thrown onto the pitch. Back home this would have been national news and those responsible would face prison terms and lengthy football banning orders. But this was Sarajevo and the players just used the stop in play to draw breath as a podgy fireman ran onto the pitch with a bucket of sand to extinguish the flares.

FK won 2–0 in what was a pretty nothingy game. Yet the referee and linesmen were pelted with bottles, coins and goodness knows what else as they made their way off the pitch. Police and officials had to shield them as they ran to the safety of the plastic covered tunnel. There was a venom in the crowd but no-one really to direct it at. It was as if these young men were acting out their own part in a strange, stylised performance: a theatre of hate without a victim, just the pantomime villain that is the poor referee. In his dystopian novel *1984*, George Orwell wrote about the "Two Minutes Hate". Every morning, party members gathered together to vent their hatred of an imaginary enemy shouting abuse at a single figure on a huge screen. It was a daily outlet for the people's anger and frustration. Has football become our weekly Ninety Minutes Hate?

These young men, and some women, on the terrace of the Otoka football ground, were obviously Sarajevo's 'lads', the hardcore, who just a few years ago would have been cowering

Chester in the shadow of the Hezbollah in the Beqaa Valley, Lebanon, 2001.

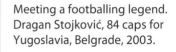

Meeting a footballing legend. Dragan Stojković, 84 caps for Yugoslavia, Belgrade, 2003.

On the way to the Land of Fire we met the Abbot at the Gelati monastery in Kutaisi, Georgia.

With Famil and Chester on our first visit to Baku, Azerbaijan.

What's the Basque for offside? Training with Koikili from Atheltic Bilbao.

Playing for peace in Nairobi, Kenya.

Playing for peace in Kenya with Stabua Khatija Yusuf of the Anyany Sisters football club, Nairobi.

Talking football, Diani, Kenya.

On top of the world with the Sámi people in Kautokeino, Norway.

Inside a Sámi lavvu near Kautokeino, Norway.

This club belongs to me! With Vincent Tan at the Cardiff City promotion party.

Chester paying homage to the Great Leader, Pyongyang, North Korea.

The Great Leader's 101st birthday, Pyongyang, North Korea.

Kicking off in North Korea – Pyongyang v Amrokkang at the Kim Il-sung Stadium.

On border duty, Panmunjom, North Korea.

Racist graffiti in Lviv, Ukraine.

Making friends at Eurofan, the football supporters' tournament in Lviv, Ukraine.

The Bulgarian supporters' team manager. 'Football, Fun, Friendship?' Lviv, Ukraine.

Firecrackers and flares at FK Sarajevo, Bosnia.

Red Star Belgrade's 'alternative' club shop.

My baptism of fire in Belgrade. Red Star v Partizan – The Eternal Derby.

Under the Scaffold with the Clapton Ultras, east London.
Picture courtesy of Claudia Krobitzsch

A fiesta in the favela, Manaus, Brazil.

Making friends at the World Cup in Salvador, Brazil.

Chester and Fatima do *Strictly* in Manaus, Brazil.

World Cup fever, Recife, Brazil.

One of the last Mayan shamans, Yucatán, Mexico.

The last day of the revolution, Maidan Square, Kyiv.

Our family holiday in Kyiv.

Стоп фашизм в России!

Flying the flag for Wales on our family holiday in Kyiv.

Antonina Dvorianets, 62. Died 18 February 2014, Kyiv.

Bedouin children at Wadi al Qteyf in the Judean desert.

Khalil Hammadeem, father, grandfather, Bedouin, Palestinian at home in Wadi al Qteyf in the Judean desert.

Peace protesters in Bethlehem, Palestine.

Leila Khaled on the 'Peace Wall', Bethlehem, Palestine.

Friday in Old Jerusalem.

Defiance in the Old City, Jerusalem.

Taking sides in the divided city of Hebron.

In the country that doesn't exist – on the streets of Tiraspol, Transnistria.

Red Dogs and Red Dragons. Matchday in Gloria Buzău, Romania.

Father and son on the pitch together.

from real munitions. Perhaps these games provide an outlet, a release of emotion and anger for all the hatred which had so recently led to murder, rape and genocide. Is football a metaphor for war? I don't know, but better this bit of play-acting than the real thing.

Richard Mills, from the University of East Anglia, has published an academic paper called 'Fighters, footballers and nation builders: wartime football in the Serb-held territories of the former Yugoslavia, 1991–1996'. He says that the outbreak of war in Yugoslavia had a devastating effect on all forms of cultural life including football. Yet in spite of the raging conflict, the game continued to be an important aspect of everyday life throughout the region.

Mills says that in the newly emerging Republika Srpska and Republika Srpska Krajina, the Serb-held territories of Bosnia-Herzegovina and Croatia, football was an important morale booster, providing soldiers with a distraction from fighting on the front. But it also served a higher cause and via league and cup competitions, it assisted in the creation of ethnically homogenous states. Alongside media coverage of the games themselves these competitions helped map the 'imagined communities' of what came to be independent nation states. Mills argues that during those war years football was being used as symbolic proof that all Serbs continued to belong to Yugoslavia. He says, "The game, and the sporting press that wrote about it, also provided an ideal subject for propaganda about enemy nations and a platform from which journalists could expound the necessities of the unification of all Serb states."

I wonder if it was our travels through the Balkans which led to Chester moving to Belgrade. I'm not sure, but two years later during that first week when we were there flat-hunting for him, the gods must have been looking down on us because it was the weekend of the football derby, Red Star versus Partizan Belgrade. They call it the Eternal Derby and we were not going to miss it.

"Get to the ground early," we'd been told and so we made our way to Zvezda (Red Star's) Marakana Stadium an hour and a half before kick-off. Police in full riot gear and helmets barred our way at the roundabout. A low but increasingly deep rumble of sound rolled down from the hill opposite. It was beastly as if dredged from the bowels of the earth. We heard them before we saw them. A dense cloud of white smoke drifted down over the trees and buildings on the hill in front of us announcing, "We are Partizan. And we are here!" As the first bottle thrown by the away fans smashed just metres from our feet I knew this was going to be a lively afternoon's football.

We could now see and hear them and we could smell the acrid smoke of the flares. Partizan's Ultras, the Grobari, were dressed to a man in black as they turned the corner onto the roundabout. They cranked up the volume, and just as in Sarajevo there was a continuous, intimidating, single drumbeat. The chants and abuse were now directed squarely at us. The police had kettled them but they had a point to make. The phalanx of hatred exploded again with a volley of bottles, sticks and flares. The shower was short-lived as the police moved them on and up towards the ground. The policy was obviously one of containment. A few of the Red Star fans dashed around the snack bar to have a go. They soon scurried back, two of them nursing their faces as the police beat them back towards us.

And then... nothing. We were held for a little until the Partizan crowd had been herded into the stadium. The traffic started up again. Our suburban street went back to normal. The old couple with plastic bags carried on home. Conversations started up and we all gingerly trod over the broken glass to make our way to a football match. Honour served, no-one hurt, and on we go. Just another derby day in Belgrade.

We'd walked this same road to the stadium the previous day to buy our tickets. Outside the home terrace two groups of some twenty riot police, batons drawn, were being briefed by their commander. One young copper was twirling his stick in boredom, or anticipation. I made a mental note not to look at any of these guys in the face.

Inside the stadium the Red Star club shop sold the usual football clobber but amazingly the Ultras have their own place alongside it on the concourse. The wall had a Banksy-type mural of a supporter, his hoodie raised to shield his face, brandishing a large stick. Inside there were shirts celebrating the terrace culture, more masked faces and some babywear with our stick wielding friend on it. Babywear!

Amazingly, for one of the must-see derby games in world football this was not a sell-out. We showed a driving licence and bought the £4 tickets. I was confused. How did they know that we were not Partizan fans going into the wrong end to make trouble? Inside the ground Chester and I peered through the fences to see yet more riot police being drilled on how to form a line down the side of the empty seats.

"Segregation," I said all knowingly. "To beat them back?"

"Or us," said Chester with a smirk.

Having listened to the advice from the ticket office we made it to the ground early and spent an hour basking in the last of the summer sunshine. The Eternal Derby? Apart from our noisy introduction to Partizan it was all rather unremarkable, but as kick-off approached things moved up a gear. A youngster pulled his hoodie over his head and climbed the heavy fencing at the corner of the stand. He produced a black Partizan shirt, hung it on the fence and set light to it. As the flames rose the crowd whooped its approval. A photographer jigged around trying to get that one shot of the fans shimmering behind this glowing symbol of hatred. And the police and stewards? They just watched from a safe distance. As did the fire officers who were stationed every ten yards or so on the running track around the field. "Just kids letting off steam," I could almost hear them say. The action was off the field of play so I guess it was alright by them.

Five o'clock finally came and the players were greeted with a massive banner which was rolled backwards from the front row over the supporters' heads. It showed a tiger biting a zebra. I guess the black and white zebra was Partizan and the tiger, er, Red Star. As the game kicked off, we held up small sheets of red and white plastic which had been stuck to our seats to form a massive tifo (a human mosaic). Giant flags were waved from the centre of the stand and the crowd sang non-stop for the whole of the first half.

Vieira (no, not the Arsenal player of old) fired Red Star ahead with a delightful chip. The crowd went mad. Then Alen Stevanović equalised for the visitors just before half-time. As if on cue, white flares were lit across the bottom of the Partizan terrace. The sun had dipped below the stand and the smoke mushroomed down to the goal, onto and then across the pitch towards us. Reflected in the floodlight, the slow-motion wave of dirty fluff was coming to get us. The bulging cotton wool cloud blotted out the pitch but we could hear the referee's whistle. It was a single, sharp blow. The game was being stopped. The referee gestured to both sets of players, directing them, not to the dressing room, but to the dugouts. I guess it must be the norm. The opposition fans get to say they stopped the game. We wait a little bit until the smoke clears and normal service is resumed. Which is exactly what happened.

Both sides had missed several good chances but that seemed to set us up for an explosive second half. And indeed the ground erupted after Vieira restored Red Star's lead with a superb volley with the outside of his foot from twenty-five metres leading to another demonstration of joy, passion and pyrotechnics. It was a cauldron of sight and sound and yet at no point did I feel threatened. Yes we were 'with our own' but there was never any danger from the opposition's shouts and flares. They were more than a hundred metres away from us and we had a near battalion of riot police to keep us apart.

There was though a group of Partizan fans at the far end of the stand to our left, away from the main body of their supporters and outside the heavy police cordon. They sang and gesticulated towards us but were only separated from the Red

Star fans, who filled most of that side of the pitch, by a thin line of stewards. They could have easily broken the cordon and got to us. But they didn't. Despite the threats and gestures they seemed happy to play their part in this noisy drama from the sidelines.

Red Star's Ultras are known as the Delije (Heroes). Formed in 1989 as part of the upsurge in Serbian nationalism in this part of Yugoslavia, the Delije brought together the various hooligan groups. Some of them claim that it was in fact they who sparked the Yugoslav war in 1990 following a violent clash with Dinamo Zagreb fans just months after the first multiparty elections in Croatia. The self-proclaimed Heroes take pride in their involvement in the war. A paramilitary battalion of Delije fought in both Croatia and Bosnia. Inside and outside the Marakana stadium, the walls are covered in murals. Red Star's Ultras vie with with Partizan's Grobari in a new war, a graffiti war, across the city of Belgrade.

When Red Star scored their third goal, midfielder Aleksandar Katai making a solo run and hitting a stinging low finish, Partizan knew the game was up. It was celebration time in our end. On seventy minutes, as if on a pre-arranged but silent signal, the Red Star fans lit their flares. The man next to me drew his hood tightly over his face. As he lit the plastic tube he tapped the guy next to us on his shoulder to move him aside. He did this very gently, respectfully almost. Our man was keen that no-one got caught in the sparkles and went home with holes in their shirt. His thick sparkler jumped into glittering life and we all moved a step away so that he was silhouetted in his own white light.

On the final whistle the jubilant Red Star players ran towards our terrace. They linked arms and bowed before us in honour of the fans. The Delije ringleader who had been marshalling our chants throughout the game threw the megaphone over the fence to the captain who joined in, rallying his teammates. This went on for a good ten minutes. And then there was quiet. That was that.

As we trooped out of the Marakana there was no singing or chanting, certainly no stone-throwing or hooliganism. The fans' anger had been contained wholly within the stadium. A young man with a shaved head and one of those nasty T-shirts with a fearsome face on it bumped into me. He stepped aside quickly and apologised profusely. He could have eaten me for breakfast. It was all rather strange. Gone were the bloodcurdling threats and the hand gestures, the synchronised chanting and the burning of shirts. We were an orderly crowd making our way home from the theatre.

I am not so naïve as to think that these fans do not hate one another. Both the kick-off and the second half of that April's Eternal Derby were delayed by smoke bombs. Thirty-five police were injured and forty-five supporters arrested following running battles inside and outside the ground.

Many of the Delije we met on our visit to the Marakana were about my age, old enough to have fought in the Bosnian wars of the early 1990s. Some of them definitely did. They tell us not to mix sport and politics, but Saturday afternoons like this, in Sarajevo or Belgrade, may have become an acceptable outlet for anger, an army reunion perhaps, definitely a chance to wave the flag and make a noise. Was the Eternal Derby unwittingly saying, 'We're all safe in a wholly Serbian republic. Let's just shout our rage out rather than fight each other.' I don't know. But I will tell you, with only a little bit of shame, that the Eternal Derby was one of the most exhilarating sporting occasions I have ever witnessed.

Albania's twenty-first-century shame

September 2013

"Blood feuds?" said Marsida as she held her coffee cup just below her lip. "Sure they still go on. It's a big deal here and of course it's the children who suffer most of all." I'd been wary of asking about blood feuds, fearing they were Albania's dirty secret. It was awkward. You want to know whether killing children is frowned upon but somehow accepted in some backward, rural areas, but how to ask? I feared my reticence was hiding a liberal, cultural relativism. The 'that's the way they do things here' and 'who are we to judge?' argument. But I needn't have worried. Marsida Cela who runs the Children Today charity seemed more than willing to fill me in as we chatted in the shaded garden of our hostel in downtown Tirana. Our Gôl! drive to Macedonia where Wales were playing had brought us from Sarajevo through Montenegro and over the high mountains to Albania. Children Today was our penultimate visit. Marsida told us that, no, blood feuds are not confined to wild rural hamlets. They happen in towns and cities too. She explained how a dispute between families can lead to murder setting in train a cycle of bloody revenge which is passed down through the generations. And caught in the middle of all this are the children.

Marsida told us the horrific story of Marsela, a nine-year-old girl who now lives in hiding in Shkodër in northern Albania. Marsela can't go to school or go out to play with her friends – for fear of being killed. She's an innocent victim of a family blood feud. Eighteen years ago her father got blind drunk and shot a friend. That set off a string of retaliatory killings which have left five people dead.

"Hang on," said Chester. "Didn't we drive through Shkodër yesterday? I'm sure we did."

"Yes, you would have done," said Marsida. "It's on the main road south here to Tirana."

Shkodër is a town of a hundred thousand people, a university town. Chester was shocked. I was shocked. The town had seemed so normal, a bit busy, downbeat, yes. It didn't look violent. But then which city does?

I took a sip of my coffee, looked at Chester and thought of him at nine years old, in that dreadful purple and yellow school uniform on a frosty school yard at half-eight in the morning. He would walk through the gates for a few yards and then look over his shoulder to see if I was still there, take a couple more paces and look back again. I'd wave and smile reassuringly but wouldn't leave until he was out of sight and safely inside the warm school hall. Then one day he didn't look back at all. I think I cried. I sometimes felt a little guilty leaving him there before the headmistress arrived, but I never feared for his safety. My son as part of a blood feud? Someone waiting at the suburban school gates to kill him? No. No, I couldn't imagine it. This was 2013, for goodness sake. But Marsida told us that in the northern area around Shkodër alone 120 children like little Marsela are living in isolation because of blood feuds. No school, no outdoor games, no waiting alone on a winter morning for Mrs Jones, the headmistress, to open up.

Men in Albania abide by a centuries-old code of law called the Kanun, which says that a murder in the family must be avenged in blood. The Kanun was an oral system, codified in the fifteenth and only written down in the nineteenth century. Book 10 section 3 (yes, it's that detailed) specifies how murder is supposed to be handled, which often leads to blood feuds that last until all the men of the two families involved are dead.

I hadn't been sure what to expect from Albania. But it was certainly not this. Apparently it has the highest concentration of guns in the world, not that we had seen one. In my youth I remember the country at the edge of Europe as the personal fiefdom of communist hardliner, Enver Hoxha. It was a hermit state which shunned even the Soviet Union for being too soft. All I knew was that life there was tough and that the only relief came from the black-and-white comedy films of Norman Wisdom, the political correctness of which Hoxha himself had okayed. Only after the communists had been overthrown and democracy brought in did we hear about the blood feuds. It was difficult to balance this grim story of medieval 'justice' with the modern and very twenty-first-century city I saw about me.

Tirana is a smart, cosmopolitan and self-confident capital. It wasn't drab or grey as I had imagined. A massive socialist realist mosaic depicting revolutionary peasants, workers and soldiers surging forward into battle still dominates the central Skanderbeg Square. It positively sparkles in bright reds, blues and greens. There was a campaign to take the mosaic down because of its communist links but common sense prevailed and it's been retained as part of Albania's architectural and historical heritage.

"See over there," said Marsida with pride pointing across the handsome tree-lined Rruga Myslym Shyri Boulevard.

"That's where the politburo used to live. That whole area. You'll pass Hoxha's own house. That's where you'll now find all the restaurants and bars. It's really nice."

Despite the shiny new shops and fancy restaurants in the capital city there are still chronic problems in Albania. Thirty-four per cent of children under the age of five suffer from stunted growth through malnutrition and despite high enrolment levels, secondary school attendance rates are only forty per cent for boys and girls. A quarter of five to fourteen year olds are actually working rather than studying.

And then of course, there are the blood feuds. Whole families are left destitute or at best isolated when the main breadwinner is forced to flee the village for his own safety. Official figures show that more than two hundred people have died in feuds over the last fourteen years, though some say the real figure is much higher.

Marsida Cela is doing her bit to try to protect the children. She trained as a social worker, studied in America and now runs Children Today. The charity has been particularly active in Shkodër advocating children's rights and running education and health programmes.

"These blood feuds are barbaric and it's got to stop," she says. "It's not easy. They're a deeply engrained part of our culture. But we do what we can."

Some believe that there was a breakdown of law and order in the early 1990s after the communist system collapsed, and that only then did people resort to the traditional ways of resolving conflicts. During a crisis in 1997 many Albanians plundered the army's weapons depots. Only a small number of the firearms was ever recovered. Albert Rakipi, writing in the *Tirana Times*, said that because of its history and isolation, the process of trying to get a functioning liberal democracy in Albania, "will go on for generations".

The government has vowed to act and has mooted a law which would raise the sentence for a blood feud killing from twenty-five to a minimum of forty years' imprisonment. We'll have to see whether the threat of a long prison stretch can break a code of honour and a cycle of behaviour which has been passed down through generations of Albanians. But any such change can't come soon enough for little Marsela as she sits at home in Shkodër dreaming about going back to school and playing with her friends.

***

Since our visit to Albania, the penalty for blood feud murder has been increased. The state, which has been given the go-ahead to apply for European Union membership, still plays down the issue saying that the number of such murders is decreasing every year. So far, so good, though I am not sure that the lure of European structural funding or agricultural subsidies will be enough to wipe out generations of barbaric tradition.

Independence, plastics and the biggest brand in the world

March 2014

IT WAS A long shot really. I was working in Barcelona and on impulse asked the hotel receptionist in my cronky Castilian, *"¿Hay entradas para el partido de Barça esta noche, por favor?"* Barcelona's Camp Nou is a must see for any football fan. Tonight they were playing at home to Celta Vigo, and we were in luck. Without hesitation from behind the desk Juliet proceeded to rattle off a price list. I could have been asking for a ticket to see *Cats* or an open top bus tour or a visit to the London Dungeon. "€100 for 'lateral' view, €65 for the lower terrace. *¿Sí?*" she said nonchalantly but thinking, 'Tourists.' I pulled a face of surprise. She ran her finger further down the page and I plumped for the cheap seats, in the gods behind the goal. A snip at €45, eh?

Two hours later Juliet handed me the tickets in a neat plastic envelope complete with complimentary Barcelona magazine, two postcards of the Catalan capital and a map showing how to get to the ground. We were on our way. Well, almost. My normal pre match routine usually takes in a pub near the ground and a couple of beers. Not this time though. My Nigerian colleague Abdulrahman, Abdul for short, had to pray before we left the centre of town. "Sorry Tim. It's that time of day."

Having presumably thanked God for the surprise tickets, the normally quiet Abdul couldn't stop talking on the metro. "Barça has always been my team. Really. Since I was little you know. And now they have Messi and all. I can't believe I am going to see them live," he said and then repeated to himself more than once in apparent disbelief, "Live."

Barcelona is no ordinary team. Founded in 1899 by a group of Swiss, English and local footballers, the club has become a symbol of Catalan culture and pride. Its motto is '*Més que un club*' (More than a club). Superlatives about Barça abound. It is the most successful Spanish team of all time and the best attended club in the world. Despite having a turnover of more than US$600million, the supporters are said to own and operate Barcelona. Its distinctive purple and blue colours are worn across continents and there are 1,335 officially registered fan clubs around the world.

The Sunday before we had arrived in the city, Barça had beaten Real Madrid in a thrilling seven-goal match and brought themselves right back into contention for the La Liga title. The animosity between Madrid and Barcelona, indeed between the Spanish state and the Catalan nation, runs deep. The club's long-standing rivalry with Real (the match between them is known as *El Clásico*) has the added edge that one team represents the capital of imperial Spain, the other a seven and a half million strong nation with its own language and culture which feels downtrodden and wants to break away from Madrid. On 14th of June 1925 the Barça crowd jeered the Spanish national anthem in a spontaneous protest against Miguel Primo de Rivera's dictatorship. The ground was closed for six months as a reprisal. During the Spanish Civil War Barcelona players fought for the Republicans and after the fascists' victory the club was forced to remove the Catalan flag from its badge. Supporting the team was a clandestine way of showing your support for the political opposition. Today it is also a demonstration of support for Catalan independence.

This club is big. Every corner of the city is draped in the

colours, scarves, flags, posters and murals of the football team. Abdul and I looked at each other and grinned as we took our seats in the dizzying heights of the Camp Nou stadium. It has a capacity of 99,787 and there are plans to increase that to 105,000. But tonight empty seats stood out on all five tiers to our right.

We had obviously been placed in the tourist section. Young Japanese girls with long dark hair, exchange students maybe, were holding nylon Barcelona flags and taking photographs. Lots of photographs. There were 'selfies', me and my friend shots, group pictures. Even Abdul got into the swing of things and made me blag a banner from the girls and snap him against the pitch way down below us. How many of these people had ever attended a football match before? Had they too read the morning paper? The headline in *La Vanguardia*, the Catalan daily, was that the Spanish Constitutional Court in Madrid had ruled the Catalan Parliament's January declaration of sovereignty as 'unconstitutional'. I also couldn't quite work out how the club as an expression of national identity could reconcile itself with also being a hugely successful international brand. Perhaps the next ninety minutes would offer some clues.

There was an excited buzz of chatter across the ground as play got underway. Barça dominated Celta from the word go. The Brazilian superstar, Neymar, scored the first goal after just six minutes. There were celebrations of sorts but the young students had missed it all. They were still busy snapping pictures with their backs to the action. They didn't seem that bothered. Abdul stood up in his seat and peered through his phone at the game. He slowly moved it to the right and to the left, taking in every corner of the stadium all the while recording his own commentary. Not on the match but on the experience. "I am here at the Nou Camp watching Barça. Live! Look there is Messi on the pitch." I hope he had a good zoom facility. We were miles away.

The local Barça fans in the stand below us tried to inject

some passion. They stood together in the very bottom tier but there can't have been more than fifty of them. They clapped and chanted to the bang of a drum and every now and again they raised eight or nine Catalan flags turning the stand, well, part of it at any rate, temporarily into a sea of defiant yellow and red stripes.

On the half-hour Abdulrahman's prayer was fully answered when his boyhood hero, Lionel Messi, scored. I jumped up in anticipation of Messi's shot, punched the air and applauded loudly as the ball went in. "C'mon Barça!" But as I sat down a firm hand was placed on my shoulder. The guy behind me gestured to the pitch and then back to me.

"No stand up," he said sharply. "I miss goal."

I couldn't believe it. This was football as tourism. No passion, no belief and certainly no standing when my team for the night was about to score. Just more camera snapping from this unofficial tourist section, the pictures securing a permanent tick in the box to say "I've done the Camp Nou".

It was as if I had stood up during the second act of *Les Mis* and spoiled everyone's view of the workers as they were about to storm the barricades. This guy behind me and the chattering girls could have been anywhere in the world. It was just another excursion for them. Being there in the moment and being passionate about football was not the point. Having been there was.

As if to underscore my contempt for these sporting day-trippers, they all then got up and left the ground with twenty minutes of play remaining. The purple and blue nylon scarves would now adorn the walls of student digs for a month or so and the selfies would no doubt be beamed home via Facebook that very night. I could see the responses: "Awesome!" "Great pics." But what was it all for?

In this country we call them 'plastics', faux supporters who follow successful teams, usually from a considerable distance. Some may never actually see the team play. Man U has plenty of them, Liverpool too. Indeed any football team which has had success down the years has its share of plastics, thousands of supporters who have no affiliation with the club, live nowhere near it but who might, just might, go there once in a lifetime. (When he was small Chester would engage other children in Cardiff city centre who were wearing Man United tops. "Wow. Man U," he'd say. "I've got friends in Manchester," and without a hint of irony ask, "Which part of the city are you from?")

The clubs themselves love the plastics. Because it is they who buy the scarves and pennants, pay through the nose for stadium tours, who drink from a red-and-white mug at work, wear the replica shirt at the kids' Saturday morning training session. They build the brand and are happy to pay for the privilege. It's all about marketing, never mind to whom. Here in Catalonia though, I was confused. Wasn't this after all a fan-owned club?

Back on the pitch Barcelona were in full control. Celta Vigo huffed and puffed but then Barça scored a decisive third goal. It was a big victory in terms of goals, but the football had been so professional, so controlled that it, like the crowd, lacked any real passion. I'm not asking for a return to the blood and guts performances of the 1970s where tackles fly in and to hell with the consequences. Nor do I want to see a bunch of skinheads on every terrace to add earthy colour to my football. But this particular experience was so bland as to be boring.

Not for Abdul though, who was still on a high as we wound our way down the endless stairs to the main concourse. I took his photo, here in front of the branded fast-food stall, there beside the mini club shop and again with the stadium floodlights in the distance. I felt good for him but a little sad for myself. I too had allowed myself to be processed. I'd been given the opportunity to be a small part of the Barça brand and just like those stupid students with their stupid scarves, iPhones and cheap flags, I'd grabbed it. It had been a fine night out and I am glad to have visited the Camp Nou. But football as tourism? No thank you. Never again.

A tale of two towns

March 2014

REFLECTED IN THE small panelled windows of Huffkins Tea Rooms (established 1890), an elegant middle-aged woman bent down in her green check Barbour coat and gave the dog a small treat. He was a wire-haired fox terrier, like the toy dogs that children in the old days pushed in front of them on a metal frame and wheels. I'm not a doggy person but I instinctively bent down and patted him.

"What's his name?"

"Bruce," said the country woman righting her Robin Hood hat. (I think there was a feather in the side of it.)

"He's been very good today so we've come for a walk to town. Haven't we, Bruce?"

I patted the dog again and without knowing it I sensed that my body, set to the speed and rhythms of the city, had slowed down. I was calm, in a different place, a different country.

You don't actually go *through* Burford these days, rather you have to turn off the A40 on the very edge of Oxfordshire to find it. It is one of the most perfectly preserved of Cotswold towns. The High Street is an unplanned jumble of architectural styles. Georgian coaching inns with wide doorways are concertinaed against black-and-white Tudor shop fronts and Victorian town houses. Along its wide cobbled pavements are antique shops, a wood stove specialist, delicatessens and tasteful cafes like Huffkins.

Intriguingly, Burford has also become an alternative mecca for fashion. But the second-hand clothes shops of yesteryear stock what they now call 'retro' or 'vintage' designs. You have to duck beneath Victorian bonnets, boas and stoles as you enter the low doorways. A bell actually rings from the doorframe to alert the shopkeeper in the storeroom or the bored student behind the desk, her nose firmly buried in *Jane Eyre*. Inside you could be in a messy dressing room in *Downton Abbey* or have found your way into an Agatha Christie novel. Never mind what we townies may think, there are no qualms here about selling real animal fur. The beaver lamb coat was a snip in the sale at £800. The handmade shoes next door were the stuff of a child's imagination and the £165 price tag placed them somewhere in the mid-range. It's an expensive place is Burford. A terraced house here will set you back £350,000 and decent detached properties go for around a million. But maybe it is its exclusivity which makes it so attractive.

I walked down the hill and past the Cotswold Arms, the Bull and the Bay Tree Inn whose windows were obscured under the sagging purple wisteria, and turned into Witney Street. An open wood fire in the Angel Inn welcomed me. A mature couple were sharing a bottle of red wine with their lunch. The luxury of red wine at lunchtime. He was wearing a crisp pink shirt and a thick knitted jumper draped over his shoulders. She, a quilted blue jacket over a sensible cashmere top. They talked unselfconsciously across the room and obviously knew the barman and the lone worker sipping his lunchtime pint at the bar, his stained baggy trousers and boots somewhat jarring the cosy atmosphere.

I went for the ploughman's and a pint of Old Hooky, an English brown ale brewed in the village of Hook Norton just north of here.

"What is that creamy cheese?" I asked the foppish young waiter who Jan, my companion for our day out, had taken a fancy to. He pushed his hair back.

"Oh, you would have to ask about the one thing that isn't local," he said in fake anger. "It's a French brie, but did you like the pork pie?" He pointed at the remains of the shiny crust on my plate. "We make them ourselves."

You can map almost all of England's history through the buildings of Burford. There was an Anglo-Saxon village here but the new town really blossomed under the Normans. Between the fourteenth and seventeenth centuries Burford was important for its wool and saddle making. In 1649 during the English Civil War, the local church was used as a prison to hold the New Model Army's 'Banbury mutineers'. Some of the 340 prisoners left carvings and graffiti on the walls, which you can still see. Henry VIII's barber-surgeon, Edmund Harman, was a native of the town. But Burford's charm, its low, yellow-white stone houses with wavy tiled roofs, may have survived like this because the railway, when it came, did not come anywhere near here. Instead the town plodded on as a coaching stop and then as a market town.

Some three miles from Burford, along a winding road and across the river Windrush, lies the tiny parish of Swinbrook. Through a squeaking metal gate and around the side of St Mary's Church is the final resting place of the Mitford sisters, the clannish, competitive, society girls of the 1930s.

Nancy was the writer, Jessica the communist, Unity the Nazi who allegedly had a dalliance with Hitler, Diana the fascist who married the leader of Britain's black-shirted boot boys, Oswald Mosley, and Debo the Duchess of Devonshire. They say Diana's funeral was a hush-hush affair attended by serious-looking men in dark glasses. Her casket was outsized and local rumour has it that the remains of Sir Oswald were buried here with her. It may be Britain's only Nazi shrine, but you would have to know that in the first place, wouldn't you?

Of course there was another Mitford girl. Pamela was more of a traditional, domesticated housewife who spent most of her unremarkable life at home in Swinbrook. The other girls disparagingly referred to her simply as 'woman'. She too is buried here. The girls' graves are plain stone affairs sticking out in a row above the unkempt grass, their glittering careers, painful love lives and ferocious political arguments now behind them.

St Mary's Church itself is a fascinating place. It holds the tombs of the local gentry, the Fettiplaces who landed on these shores with William the Conqueror. Generation after generation of this noble family has outdone each other in the design and grandeur of the family tombs. Beside the altar their alabaster caskets line the wall, stacked one on top of the other in shelves, like bunk beds, the effigies resting on their elbows as if posing for a portrait painter. Country life, country death.

Back across the swollen river Windrush, the Swan Inn is something of a shrine to the Mitford girls. Grainy black-and-white pictures of hunting parties, weddings and the girls striking studied, bored poses have been blown up and mounted on the walls. It was to the Swan, 'Britain's poshest pub' as one critic snidely called it, that the Prime Minister David Cameron brought the French President François Hollande, here to his constituency, to sample a slice of 'real' England. Their picture, both raising a glass of Oxfordshire ale in another stilted pose, also now adorns the plastered walls of the Swan.

***

The next day I travelled north from Cardiff to Pontypridd, past the pithead winding gear and silent wheels at Trehafod, now optimistically reinvented as the Rhondda Heritage Museum, and on to Treorchy passing through Llwynypia, Ystrad, Gelli and Ton Pentre on the way. The villages along the floor of the valley either side of the river bleed seamlessly into one other. There's no beginning to this ribbon of post-industrialisation and no visible end. Long terraces of uniform miners' homes are punctuated here and there by massive pubs which, if they are still open, are doubling up as advertisements for Sky Sports Live and Carling Lager, the plastic banners flapping on filthy cords against the red brick walls.

I was looking for a suitable venue to screen an independent

film marking the 30th anniversary of the Miners' Strike and at the Parc and Dare Hall in Treorchy I was greeted by Simon Davey the theatre manager.

"Sorry we can't go into the lower bar area. It's ladies' aerobics on Wednesday morning," he said as he ushered me into the box office. Steve passed me a mug of hot tea and I took my place on the high swivel stool behind the glass partition. It was not much of an office but it felt quite cosy.

From the outside the Parc and Dare is a rather austere grey stone building on the corner of the High Street. Built in 1892 it was a working men's library and institute paid for by the workers of the Park and the Dare collieries. The miners saved a penny from each pound of their wages every week, testament to their desire to better themselves, to get an education, to 'get out of here' I suppose. The external style of the building was influenced by the architecture of Welsh nonconformist chapels. Driving up the valley I'd passed many examples of these bygone temples of faith. They had good Old Testament names – Nebo, Zoar, Carmel and Zion. Some are now derelict while others have been turned over to decidedly non-religious uses, carpet stores or tyre fitters. Moriah in Tonypandy actually became a curry house, the Knight of Bengal.

Simon told me a bit of the Parc and Dare's history. In 1930, the first 'talkie' picture was screened here. It was called *The Broadway Melody* and I imagined it flickering away on a Saturday night to a full house of well-scrubbed men, flat caps in hand, in awe at this new cinematic invention. But as the mines and the congregations declined so did the Parc and Dare and in 1975 it closed. The local council took pity on it and reopened the hall which today is still a working theatre and cinema. The week I was there they were staging an amateur production of *Calendar Girls*. Ray Davies of the Kinks has graced the main stage, Max Boyce too.

"I haven't been here long," said Simon. "Only eight years. Tell you what. Come back in ten minutes when the girls have finished and I'll show you around properly."

So I took a walk along another British high street. Around the corner from the Parc and Dare is Carpanini's café, one of the few 'Italians' left in the valleys. The Rossi, Minoli and Bracchi families left their villages in Emilia-Romagna in droves during the rural depression of the early twentieth century and headed to south Wales to cash in on the mining boom. I remember sipping frothy coffee here in Carpanini's in the 1970s, making it last an hour over my last, precious Benson and Hedges. They call it cappuccino now and charge an arm and a leg for it.

Treorchy is still a busy little place but the people seemed very different from those I had met in Burford. An old woman handed a blue-and-red striped plastic bag bulging with groceries to her husband as she wrestled with her walking stick. A put-upon mum stopped her double buggy in the doorway to the sports shop, checked the babies and took a look at the replica Wales rugby shirts. No, they're far too big for them at the moment. There was plenty of chat along the plain grey pavement but the people were dressed practically, in brown or grey overcoats, their hoods up against the cold wind rushing down the valley. I saw a dog here too but this one was a Staffordshire bull terrier straining at the leash. This time I didn't engage his young male owner in conversation.

Where Treorchy's High Street becomes Bute Street I noticed more charity shops than I saw in Burford and there was a Stardust gambling arcade, which I certainly didn't see the previous day. In place of the vintage clothes shops with their canopy of fox furs and sparkling 1920s accessories this town had nail centres, hairdressers and the obligatory tattoo parlour. But there are some real gems too. Morris Family butchers has a fine shop front and window display. The homemade faggots looked fantastic – plump and dimpled, dark brown and heavily glazed sitting temptingly on a massive stainless steel tray. And around the corner is the cheekily named chip shop, A Fish called Rhondda. I stopped at the Shoe Zone and peered in through the broad single pane window framed in stainless steel. Nothing cost more than fifty quid. The houses are dirt cheap here too. A two-up two-down in Dumfries Street will set you back just £61,000.

Back at the Parc and Dare the ladies aerobics was over and women of all shapes and ages in lycra tops and pink and grey running bottoms, gossiped over their bottled water as they packed their things away. But as he showed me around the auditorium with its two fine curved galleries, Simon became a bit downbeat.

"They're cutting our funding you see. The council. It's all a bit grim. I don't think they'll shut us down, maybe just close one or two of the public areas. We can't afford to run them all. Pity really. The girls really love it here. But you never know."

East London's noisy revolution

April 2014

THERE'S A REVOLUTION going on in east London. It's loud, colourful and slightly edgy, but I doubt you'll have heard about it. Because gritty Forest Gate in the London borough of Newham is hardly the first place you would look for it. Hidden behind a rather run-down tyre fitters, the only sign of the uprising is a crumbling wooden sign which reads "Clapton Football Club".

Inside the Old Spotted Dog ground, the battlefield is a threadbare football pitch. Clouds of dust were blowing up as I watched the players warm up. The nets were ancient and the linesman wore a cardigan, long trousers and trainers. The proper official had been caught in the Tube strike.

But as soon as the game kicked off, so did the Clapton Ultras. Red smoke bombs blotted out the pitch and a bizarre version of 'When the Saints Go Marching In' rattled off the roof of the tiny terrace: "Oh, east London is wonderful. Oh, east London is wonderful. It's full of pies, mash and Clapton. Oh, east London is wonderful." A hundred or so supporters had squeezed under a dodgy roof of corrugated sheets held up by a pile of rusting scaffold poles. The self-proclaimed 'Scaffold Brigada' have turned Clapton games into a riot of colour, noise, tins of lager and general good times.

Chester was living in London and had thrown his lot in

with Clapton FC. His contempt for professional football and the modern game had led him to this allegedly more authentic sporting experience. "This is what it's all about," he'd enthused. "Not big stars on ridiculous money, all-seater stadiums, bolshie stewards and police restrictions. Forget all that branding and replica shirt stuff. The real thing is down there in Clapton. Football's not dead. Honest. You've got to come see it for yourself, Dad." And so I did.

Today's opponents were Eton Manor and their eleven players had not seen anything like this in the Essex Senior League. Neither had I, for that matter. As their keeper stepped gingerly through the thick grass and nettles behind the goal to retrieve the ball another chant swept across the ground. "RMT, RMT, RMT" to the tune of 'Here We Go' rang out in praise of the transport workers' union which had crippled the London Underground that day. This was closely followed by a full rendition of Billy Bragg's anthem 'Power in a Union'. Because, you see, these Ultras are not of the skinhead fascist variety. Quite the opposite in fact.

John Venners, dressed in a duffle coat with a rolly cigarette hanging from his lip, waved a flag with "Anti-Fascist Alliance" hand painted in red and white on a black background. Another home-made banner read "Sometimes anti-social. Always anti-fascist". For this is a very leftist, 'right on' kind of a crowd and they don't care who knows it. These wannabe revolutionaries wear their hearts on their sleeves and those hearts are firmly on the Left. Rumour had it that the local English Defence League thugs would come down to 'sort out the Commies,' but nothing so far had happened.

John had tried to hand me a flag to wave but as this was my first time I didn't want to appear to be jumping on the bandwagon. In my 1970s heyday we had all manner of political causes to shout about. General Pinochet, gay rights, apartheid and the 'occupation' of Ireland. Blair Peach had been beaten to death by the Met, Maggie was in power and the Welsh language was dying on its feet. This generation was supporting Clapton

FC and, erm... the transport workers' union of course. How times change.

There was a whiff of Spitalfields chic about the grungy beards, duffle coats and combat trousers on parade. This was designer Red before the fashion houses clocked it and the labels moved in. Lapels bore anti-fascist and FC St Pauli insignia. (The German club is renowned for its anti-Nazi stance.) Bohemian, maybe. Trendy, certainly. It all had a distinct 'hipster' element to it. My journalist friend Ade had also had a taste of the Clapton experience but he was a little sceptical about it all. "Hmm," he said. "It seems a bit post-student to me. Let's see how many of them are down the Old Spotted Dog in three years' time." But take away the politics and it is football as entertainment, Ade. Isn't that what it's supposed to be all about?

Clapton were 2–0 down within twenty minutes but the fans didn't care. Up went a chorus reviling Maggie Thatcher and praising Tony Benn. At last, something I could relate to! Someone used the c-word in a chant. A bald-headed young man from the back shouted loudly but politely, "Come on, guys, didn't we agree last week not to use that word?"

"Yeah, right," came a voice of support from behind the Scaffold. And the chant stopped dead.

This level of support is pretty remarkable given that Clapton were in the ninth tier of English football and the players are not paid. The 'Tons' ended the season in the wilderness known as the middle of the table. But how to explain the fanatical support from the wobbly terrace? Are the Ultras a grassroots movement revolting against modern football, its obsession with money and the marginalisation of the real fan? Or is it just a fad? The latest trendy way of raising two fingers to the world, a safe form of leftist gesture politics?

Oddly, Clapton's owner is not too pleased with the attention his team is getting. The fans have started asking questions about how the club is structured and financed. I was warned, in the nicest possible way, not to buy my beer in the clubhouse.

"Don't give him anything. He won't put it back into this club," I was told. I didn't dare ask who 'he' was. The assistant coach, Neil Day, had recently been sacked for being 'too close' to the club's supporters. At the first match after his dismissal, the Ultras unveiled a banner supporting him. Chester pointed Day out to me and waved. He came across, smiled warmly and shook my hand in a warm welcome. Despite his demotion he's still a big fan of the club and is happy to continue to cheer his lads on from under the Scaffold.

On the way to the ground Chester had introduced me to Dave. He works in the Oxfam shop in Victoria. "But I did go to university," he added quickly. Dave's from Lincoln and started following the Tons a year ago. "I don't know why," he said. "Maybe it's the history of the ground. Did you know it's the longest continually used senior football ground in London? I've tried 'proper' football but I'm hooked on this lot now. You really feel a part of something here."

There's no doubting the closeness of the players and the fans. Together they designated a game at Tower Hamlets as a fundraiser for homeless charities. The Tons' right winger Billy Wise was on the streets at sixteen but found a way out with the help of football. He's played for and coached the England homeless World Cup side. Players and fans united. That day in Tower Hamlets was International Women's Day and the fans unveiled a giant banner which read "Real Ultras are Feminists". It also inspired perhaps the oddest chant of all time. To the tune of 'Yellow Submarine' they sang, "We all live in a patriarch regime, a patriarch regime, a patriarch regime."

My game ended in a 3–1 defeat but the result counted for nothing. The crowd went berserk anyway. The Tons' captain, Craig Greenwood, was carried precariously, shoulder high from the pitch towards, where else, the sacred Scaffold. He was beaming. Cue more flares, fists pumping the air, the throwing of beer and chanting. All the players stayed on the pitch for an impromptu end of season party.

The manager Chris Wood made an impassioned speech. "We can't pay these lads money," he said. "You know that. But you guys…"

"And girls," came a shout from the back.

"Er, and girls," he continued. "Your support is brilliant. People have heard about you lot all the way up to the Ryman League. Teams hate coming here and the celebration you give my players when they score, well, that's what I can offer them. Please, please keep it up next season."

The next challenge for the Clapton Ultras is to try to take ownership of their club. Never mind the RMT and Tony Benn. Forget the imminent victory of international socialism for a minute. If the Ultras can take control of Clapton FC, then this ragbag revolution in east London could really be going somewhere.

(The names of the Clapton supporters have been changed at their request.)

Pride and privilege

May 2014

YOU ARE TO remain silent as you walk down the Marble Corridor. And as they paraded slowly along the black-and-white tiles on the eastern side of the college building the young ladies of Cheltenham were indeed seen and not heard. We adults too, in deference to this most English of educational institutions, spoke only in hushed tones. For this was The Cheltenham Ladies' College. Founded in 1854 it was to be "an institution for the daughters and young children of noblemen and gentlemen". And so it has been ever since.

Mum was eighty-eight, recently diagnosed with cancer and, well, slowing up a little. Over the years she had spoken with affection of her days at Cheltenham, its brilliant students, quirky ways and dreamy corridors. So I thought a visit there would give her a bit of a boost as she awaited those dreadful non-academic 'results'.

We entered the College from the main road through St George's archway. The heavy wooden door clunked behind us and after a few echoing steps we emerged into the light of the quad, and into another, closed, world. We were greeted by Caroline Harris, a doughty woman in her forties who sported a gold badge bearing the title, Alumni Relations Officer. Mum strained to see her old house, Fauconberg, at the far end of the quad. Girls passed us hurriedly on their way to the science block, the youngsters chatting animatedly, the older girls looking rather more serious, hugging bundles of books.

"What are they wearing?" asked Mum, squinting with her failing eyes.

"Blue-and-green kilts and blue shirts," I told her, "but the older ones are wearing trousers."

"Trousers?" she said under her breath. Mum was not impressed.

"Is that a young man?" This time she almost choked. "Do they let boys in here now?" Her voice was a mix of incredulity and disappointment. "The only man we ever saw here was the music teacher, Dr Sumpsion. A lovely man. He used to smile at me. He was the organist at Gloucester Cathedral."

Caroline too smiled at Mum and reassured her that all had not been lost. "It's alright. The young man's a teacher. Maths, I think. We have quite a few male teachers here now. Definitely no boys though."

Mum had entered The Cheltenham Ladies' College for the first time in 1941. (They make a big deal of the 'The' in the college's name, though I'm not sure why.) It was wartime, but in defiance of Mr Hitler's bombs and with some months of evacuation to a local manor house, the education of England's female elite continued as normal. And despite the betrousered girls and the male teachers, you could imagine that behind the thick college walls nothing has really changed in seventy-something years.

From the quad we entered the Marble Corridor, a hundred metres long with niches in the wall holding statues of women who had given "service to humanity". We were shown into the Archive Display Room. This place has its own museum. The doctoral robes of Dorothea Beale, Cheltenham's most famous lady principal, hang next to the traditional green woollen uniform of yesteryear. There's even a film and sound archive. But Mum was more interested in the wood panels along the walls which held the names of the college's Oxbridge scholars across the years, all spelt out in uniform gold lettering. She had me read the names of her illustrious contemporaries and every now and then would sigh, "She had a brilliant mind. Oh, she was a lovely girl. Good at lacrosse too."

The College has a former pupils' association known as the Guild, and every so often mum receives an update on who's done what and where the glittering gals are now. The recent alumni are very busy, research neurologists, diplomats and academics. The older ones are still contributing though in rather different ways these days: Paula Hinton edits the parish magazine in Stroud, Delphie Giles runs a volunteer group in Atherton, Australia. By keeping in touch like this these women, all in their eighties, are sharing a common bond, perhaps keeping a flame alive.

My finger paused on the wood panel at the name of Colette E D Clarke, who won a scholarship to Lady Margaret Hall, Oxford, in 1951. Colette was the daughter of Sir Kenneth Clarke, he of television's *Civilisation* fame, and the sister of the colourful Conservative cabinet minister, Alan Clarke. Her grandmother, Dr Winifred Martin, was a woman doctor, a rare enough thing in the 1930s. She served for a short time as a locum in the south Wales valleys in my grandfather's general practice. It was then that she told my grandmother what an amazing place Cheltenham was, that their Colette had just started as a junior, and that "you could do no better than to send Eleanor there to finish her schooling". So that was that.

Further down the Marble Corridor lies the oak-panelled main library. "I can smell it," said Mum as we neared the doorway. And she was right. It was an old-fashioned library smell, like you don't really get any more. There were books, lots of them. Twenty thousand, in fact. The stained-glass windows celebrate famous men of letters, Homer, Virgil, Shakespeare and Goethe. This world of learning had not yet been taken over by laptops and digits. It was exam time and the girls stared seriously down onto their lined notepads, fingers fiddling with highlighter pens and biros.

"It really was a rounded education," said Mum as we left the girls to their revision. "We had Greek Week when all lessons were stopped and we studied Greek art, literature and philosophy. A Dr Livingstone from Oxford University came to talk to us. He was marvellous. D'you know it was the first time I appreciated learning for its own sake, not just for exams." Mum was in her stride. "There was choral singing and we had outings to Stratford. They let me take English criticism alongside my science subjects. Gosh, there were some bright girls here!" And she went on to tell us about the head prefect, Lesley Stuart Taylor, and her friend Helen Lucas Tooth who both went up to Oxford to do arts and English. Mum didn't do too badly herself. She studied medicine in Edinburgh and became a consultant psychiatrist.

Just along from the library at the foot of a staircase there's a large alcove dedicated to Dorothea Beale. She gave forty-eight years of her life to the refinement of young women in Cheltenham, and on a plinth in the recess stands a bust of the great woman surrounded by an inscription lettered by Eric Gill. It is something of a shrine to the Ladies, present and past. Or so it should be.

Mum giggled as she remembered how, at the end of her last term at college, Ann Watt decorated the alcove with empty beer bottles in a simple, rebellious gesture. "How she got hold of them I'll never know," said Mum, "but Miss Popham, the principal, called us together and there was an almighty stink." Weeks later I checked this story again with my mother. She didn't giggle this time but clutched my hand. She drew me close and whispered earnestly, "You won't name Ann, will you? Just in case. You know." There was my Mum back as a nervous schoolgirl in 1943.

The visit had taken her back seventy years. She was remembering names, dates and events and was feeling rather mischievous herself. "We had a very naughty poem about Miss Beale and another rather prim teacher, Miss Buss. Would you like to hear it?" She didn't wait for an answer. *"Miss Buss and Miss Beale, Cupid's darts do not feel. How different from us, Miss Beal and Miss Buss."* Such innocence.

Not that Mum had been an absolute angel there either. Mrs Churchill had started a fund to raise money to buy warhorses for the Russians and the Young Ladies were expected to do their bit. During 'Energies Week' the girls would charge each other a small fee for doing odd jobs, cleaning your shoes, mending clothes or whatever. The funds were then sent to Mrs Churchill who presumably passed the bundle on to Mr Stalin to buy his horses. Mum decided that she would help her colleagues with their homework. She charged 3d for a Latin prose and 6d for a French translation. It all went very well and she ended up raising more money than anyone else. In fact it was such a good thing that she decided to carry on even after Energies Week had ended. Never mind the war effort and Stalin's horses, she was now pocketing the money for herself, until the English mistress noticed some striking similarities in the girls' essays on Penguin books, which had become popular at the time. The unthinkable happened – Mum was sent to Miss Popham.

"These girls' parents are paying a lot of money for their education," said the principal. "How do you think they would feel if they knew that you were doing their homework?"

"But if they let me do it then they're not really worth all that money are they?" said my unrepentant mother.

"That will do," ordered Miss Popham and that was the end of that.

As we left the Marble Corridor I touched the wall and held my hand on its cold surface. Was I hoping that it would somehow connect me with the past, allow me, however briefly, to share an idyllic, dreamy boarding school experience I had read about and seen in countless films? Rarefied, privileged, my young and innocent mind a blank page being opened up to limitless possibilities through 'good' books and careful direction. An independent mind yes, but also one imbued with a sense of duty and obligation. I could see a corridor of doors, all slightly ajar. None was closed and everything was possible. Life as a blank slate waiting to be written on.

Mum interrupted my thoughts. "You couldn't fail in a place

like this though, could you?" she said. We thanked Caroline profusely and posed for photographs before the ivy-clad music and drama wing. Two Chinese girls stepped aside politely allowing us to pass on the footpath. I had noticed a number of non-European faces as we'd passed through the college.

"Do you have many foreign students here?" I asked Caroline.

"Yes, we have," she said, "but we do keep an eye on numbers. You know, so as not to lose sight of things."

On the way home I asked Mum why she hadn't sent me to a school like this.

"Well, there were four of you kids," she said. "We just couldn't afford it." There was a pause before she added as if to herself, "Mind you, it's wrong, isn't it? Public schools and privilege, Cameron and that lot. All the same, aren't they? Eton and Oxbridge. No, it's wrong. I don't think I could have done it. Even if I'd had the money. Really."

The 'independent' school had bred an independent mind. Well done, Mum. Well done, Cheltenham.

A fiesta in the favela

June 2014

I'D JOKED WITH Chester that he'd get his first taste of tear gas in Brazil. But it was not to be. We'd seen the television images of young men in masks throwing firebombs in Rio and São Paulo. Brazil may have won the right to host the football World Cup but the whole country was supposedly in revolt. Anti Fifa, anti-government, anti-slum clearance. By the time we reached Manaus in the Amazonas province the protestors seemed to have all disappeared. Our fears however, had not.

The hotels were full for the football. We had just managed to get a double bed to share in a private house and from the airport we made our way to the home of Mara Costa. The taxi turned off the main road into the city and up a hill into a maze of increasingly narrow and shabby streets. It was early afternoon and the sun was bright and hot. The taxi slowed on yet another street with no name. Two black chickens picked their way through the dirt, ragged children played football in the gutter and a mangy dog with distended teats lay down and scratched its bald patch. Hadn't we been this way before? Who knows? We were lost.

The car slowed down at the bottom of a steep dip in another street for the umpteenth time. The driver wound down his window and again asked the way. A young man sat impassively on a low stool and stared at us both in the back of the air-conditioned car. It was the tattoos which first caught my eye. A snake in deep blue, red and green wrapped itself around his upper body, the eyes bulging on his broad shoulder. Lifeless on his light brown skin, but seemingly ready to bite. The man wiped the sweat off his forehead with a blue handkerchief and shook his head.

"No numbers here," said the taxi driver agitatedly, and then started an awkward three-point turn in the narrow street. On the opposite side of the alley another man looked up from the chrome of the motorbike he was polishing. His snake, identical in style and colour to his neighbour's, wrapped itself around his right arm. He too gave us a blank look. "Gangs," I said to Chester, "where the hell are we?" I didn't try to hide my fear.

This was Redenção, a poor suburb of Manaus, a favela, the downbeat neighbourhood for the downtrodden people whose only hope, if the papers back home were to be believed, was to rob each other and push drugs. The World Cup was going to be a bonanza for them too. Foreigners, gringos with dollars, and lots of them. Every piece of advice we'd been given had said, "Stay away! Whatever you do, avoid the favelas!"

Impossibly conspicuous, me in white chinos and check shirt, Chester in a bright red Wales football shirt and Ray-Bans, we got out of the car and hammered on the metal shutters. Every home here is its own gated community, every window barred, the walls topped with vicious metal spikes and razor wire. The dog barked as Mara Costa rattled back the heavy metal door and ushered us into her home. We were safe at last.

"Dangerous?" Mara answered us, almost in disbelief. "No, no, no, no, no. I walk here on my own. No problem. Safe, yes safe." Mara and her family were cashing in on the World Cup and had thrown their home open to visitors. We were sharing the house with no name – it was actually Rua Independência, 44A, not that it had helped – with Carlos from Honduras and a group of twenty-something Americans. Emma was on a gap year. Her cousin Frank, who had some issues with his father in Philadelphia which he was rather too keen to talk about, was on what he called a "gap life". There were other relations too, but I couldn't work out who belonged to who. They all seemed to squeeze into one large bedroom and would emerge in dribs and drabs in various states of undress. We'd all come to Manaus to visit the Amazon. The Americans had the bonus of supporting their national team and, since Wales had not qualified for the World Cup finals since 1958, Chester and I were there to support, well, football. Mara's house was functional if a little crowded and her welcome was in stark contrast to what we'd been led to expect.

Manaus was the last stage of our three-week tour of six Brazilian cities so I guess if we were going to get trapped in a riot or robbed at gunpoint then we had given the gangs and the druggies ample opportunity to do so. Yes, we did get followed by a car in Salvador. It was late at night and everything was shuttered up. The back window was wound down and a young man looked up and down the street as the car moved very, very slowly. Slightly scary, but nothing actually happened. Neither was Salvador, the well-preserved colonial seaport, the hell-hole João, in whose flat we had stayed in Brasília, had described. He'd seen pregnant young girls smoking crack on the cobbles of the old town and had woken up one morning to find a body under his hotel balcony. Each city in Brazil told us a bad story about our next port of call. As we'd clambered out of our hire car in picture postcard Olinda in the north-west Pernambuco province, a woman in a sleek black Mercedes pulled up alongside us. She gestured at our bags and told us to mind our backs. Why were the people so angry? Why were we apparently in permanent danger? Was it poverty, inequality and a government mortgaging the nation's future for the sake of a month-long sporting jamboree? Take your pick.

We'd been told that the footballing *cartel* – literally 'top hats' in Portuguese, those who run the domestic game in Brazil – were in hock with the politicians and that they were all in one way or another making a fortune on the back of the World Cup. The people we met though seemed resigned to it all. There's an expression in Brazil, *"Ele rouba mas faz"*, which roughly translates as "He steals but he gets things done". So that's OK, then.

In Recife we'd got chatting to Daniel Cabral, a young photographer. "What do people really think of the World Cup?" Chester asked him. "Do they say it's all a waste of money?"

Daniel paused before answering. "Our public services and schools are in a poor state," he said. "That's true. But it's not just in Rio, you know. There were protests here in Recife too. Yes. Riots and tear gas and all that. Terrible. But now we are all behind the national team."

The next afternoon Mara was in a hurry. Chester and I were still dazed from the riot of colour and sound we had encountered outside the Manaus Opera House the previous night. A 'Fan Zone' had been erected with big screens showing football, street vendors sold drinks and music from three different bands competed across the square for our attention. We were also still stunned at being in the bosom of our new and extended family.

"Come on or we'll be late," Mara shouted as she went from room to room, banging on doors. The Costa family were taking us to see the match. It was Brazil versus Cameroon and we'd been invited to a neighbour's to watch it on a big screen. Emma and Frank, the Americans, appeared laden with tins of beer and draped necklaces of plastic beads in red white and blue around my neck. Carlos the Honduran produced a bottle of rum, shook it at us and grinned wildly. Together this gonzo United Nations team walked noisily and carelessly through those same streets which just twenty-four hours earlier had held such fear for Chester and me.

Along the way families were settling onto the porch around television screens. The schools were closed for the day and there was a party atmosphere as old and young, men and women, came together in support of the *Canarinhos* (the Canaries) as the national side is affectionately known. As we passed the ramshackle homes the Americans shouted, *"Brasil! Brasil!"* The children waved and sounded their plastic horns. The adults raised their glasses and shouted back at us.

The houses and shops were bedecked in yellow-and-green

bunting and every here and there Brazilian flags fluttered on poles. We went through another heavy gate and were greeted with hugs by Fatima and her friends. Her back yard was dominated by a huge widescreen telly hanging against the wall under a makeshift awning. A scrawny dog was tied with a chain in the corner of the yard. One of the young Americans went over and made a fuss of him as we settled into our plastic seats.

Fireworks and fog horns rang out across Redenção as the game kicked off. Brazilians for the day, we cheered every pass and booed every foul. After ten minutes piles of chips with rock salt, olives, lumps of cheese and little nibbles of fried beef were produced. We processed back and forth to the fridge for tin after tin of beer. It was an amazing show of generosity by people we had never met before. I lit a Cuban cigar and drew on it heartily. The Americans were almost in awe. "Is that Cuban? I mean really Cuban?" said Hank and they took pictures of each other 'breaking' their country's trade embargo against the communist state as they puffed on the forbidden tobacco.

Inevitably, Brazil scored and big Luiz, who had been sitting on a deckchair in his baggy vest at the back of the yard, picked up the bottle of rum, turned it upside down above his head and noisily glugged a hefty measure. He slammed the bottle down and in imitation of the excited television commentators screamed, "*Goooooool!*" We all whooped our approval. This mayhem was repeated at every one of Brazil's four goals. The party was in full swing and it was still only mid-afternoon.

At half-time Luiz staggered over to the telly and put a DVD on. It was *Queen – Live at Wembley*. Why Queen I do not know, but the thumping beat of 'Under Pressure' lent the afternoon a slightly surreal aura. I used to think that football itself was the international language. Anywhere I went in the world I would just have to mention the name of that country's top footballer and wave my hands or clap in admiration, and bingo, we were friends for life. But no, the music of Queen is truly the international language. We all screamed with Freddie, 'I Want to Break Free' and pranced around the yard to 'Bohemian Rhapsody', clenched fists pumping the air before cooing theatrically, "Nothing really matters" to each other.

The game finally ended but this time Fatima put samba music on the big screen and we all danced in celebration of the host nation's victory. No-one was spared. Chester was being led through a strange and unseemly jive by Fatima who was old enough to be my wife and his mother. He'd looked disapprovingly at me as she had sweatily hugged me during the first dance. Ha! Now it was his turn. Fatima beat Chester's fist on her ample breast in a show of, I think, affection, and they both almost fell over as the song ended on a crashing beat. There were no inhibitions. We were all having FUN. We wriggled around each other and twisted our arms up and over as the samba became a jive. Although in their sixties, Mara and her husband Mateus could still do a fine routine. We formed a circle around them. Their performance drew applause from Chester and me, high fives from the young Americans.

The whole neighbourhood was celebrating the victory as we slowly wound our way home. At the corner of Fatima and Mara's streets we were beckoned into a pavement bar. It was a simple affair. Yellow plastic chairs and tables were set around a tiny opening in the wall where beer and food were served. The place had been painted in a dull blue and a corrugated roof of sorts offered a little shade. As we stepped over the kerbstone and into the bar people filled their glasses with beer and held them out to us to share. A portly man cut some meat from his plate and poked his fork at me urging me to eat.

"More, more," he said. Everyone wanted to talk to us and have their picture taken with these exotic new footballing friends.

After a while I spoke to the man I assumed was the barman. "Could I now buy some beer for you?"

He looked offended. "No. No. Our party. You very welcome," he said and poured yet more beer into the communal glass.

Chester and I eventually left the party. The Americans and Carlos had had enough but we wanted to go further into the favela. Darkness had fallen and we were in a bit of a daze. I think we were daring each other to venture deeper into the unknown. It wasn't going to be difficult but did we have the nerve? In no time we found ourselves in another bar. This one though was even more basic. A couple of corrugated sheets had been slung over someone's front porch. The smell of piss wafted in from the doorless, pitch-black toilet in the adjoining shack. A plastic cigarette lighter was tied to the wall with a piece of string and every so often the ill-looking couple in the corner would come across to light up. She was very thin and her skin looked translucent. He was maybe a little older and had lost his two front teeth.

"I think they're on drugs or something," I said to Chester, trying to be the adult.

"Maybe they're just poor," he said.

Emboldened by the drink Chester tried to engage the old man in a string vest sitting on his own in conversation.

"Football," he repeated animatedly. "We come here for football."

That bit the old man got but, "Wales. *País de Gales*. Next to *Inglaterra*," he did not.

"Ryan Giggs. Gareth Bale. John Charles?" Chester persevered. We drew imaginary maps with our hands pointing out Europe and the position of our little nation. Nothing. We gave up and sat in silence unsure whether we had come too far this time. Then the old man exploded. "John Charles! *País de Gales*!" He came over and shook our hands. The name of one of Wales's greatest footballers from the 1950s had jogged his memory and at last he knew where these strangers had come from.

As we finished our drinks the ill-looking couple came over and gesticulated up the hill. It was the first time they had taken any real notice of us. We'd both reached the stage of drinking where we knew we were still vulnerable but were confident enough to chance our luck in pursuit of another authentic Brazilian experience. They led us past the sanctuary of Mara's house and on again. We were leaving it, Mara and safety, behind. Chester and I looked at each other, egging each other on, neither one wanting to admit to real fear or be the one to spoil the party which refused to end.

Some 500 metres down a straggly lane we came to a bar which straddled both sides of the street corner. The back wall was adorned by a hand-painted crest enshrining the letters CRF. Our dodgy new friends had brought us to a football bar, the home of the Manaus supporters' chapter of the Rio de Janeiro team, Flamengo. It was 2 a.m. but this place was in no hurry to close. We played pool with the ill couple and made what conversation we could. Pidgin Spanish, the odd word of Portuguese, hand gestures, whatever. They too refused our money and shared their beer with us. The man left some spittle on the glass as he passed it over, but heck, what could I do? A motorbike drew up alongside the bar and a tray of eggs was lifted from the rack and placed on the bar. The group standing there waved to us to eat the freshly boiled eggs. My fingers burned as I peeled the hot shells and pinched salt and pepper over them. I stopped at two. Chester politely nibbled at his and then disappeared into the toilet.

A young man wearing a Flamengo shirt wanted his picture taken with us. He was short and podgy and had cross-eyes, grunted rather than spoke and punctuated our unintelligible conversation with big hugs and kisses. No-one else took much notice of him. The ill-looking couple were taking the pool game seriously. The toothless man paused and considered a shot while she rolled yet another cigarette. The cross-eyed lad pointed at our Wales tops and gave us the thumbs up. This we did understand. Chester and I peeled off our sweaty shirts. Chester turned his head away as he exchanged his for the lad's smelly Flamengo top. Mine was brand-new and was handed to me in a sealed plastic bag. I smirked at Chester as I ripped through the plastic and put it on. There were more photos with us grinning in our new tops. We were starting to flag and tried to say goodbye.

Even now, through a haze of beer and cigarette smoke, there was still a nagging 'but' in my mind. I kept thinking something awful was about to happen. Had we pushed the night just a little too far this time? We didn't really know the way back to Mara's. Why hadn't we heeded the advice? Surely we would get mugged at some point? But we didn't and Chester and I walked home under a half-moon with only a distant dog's bark breaking the stillness. It was a perfect moment.

Looking back now on our wild night in Redenção I feel small and peevish. These were not the gun-toting robbers we had been told to avoid. This welcome in the favela was genuine. What little these people had, they wanted to share with us, complete strangers. As we finally left the bar that night there had been thanks and hugs and that one, final picture. A chunky lad in the corner got up and came over. He squeezed my hand warmly and smiled. *"Obrigado,"* I said. "Thank you." His shirt blew open in the night breeze, flapping above his back. His arm was covered with an ugly serpent tattoo. The same one we had seen just the day before.

History People

July 2014

IT WAS NOT a holiday I would have chosen. A five-star, all-inclusive beach resort – Playa del Carmen on the Yucatán peninsula in Mexico. That's right, just down the coast from the concrete holiday monstrosity that is Cancún. But it was our twenty-fifth wedding anniversary, we wanted to do something 'different' and I was feeling in a generous mood. "It's not like what you think," Helen had said in an unassured reassuring way. "It's the centre of the Mayan culture and there are loads of temples and stuff for you. You'll really like it." And so it proved.

Over a fruity cocktail in the cavernous cocktail bar of the Riu Palace hotel, Amy, the Thomson rep who was to be our very own "friend away from home" as she put it, duly rattled through the visits and excursions on offer. She politely steered me away from hiring a car to do our own thing. In her homely sing-song Nottingham accent Amy said, "You'd be OK on the main roads but the police will stop you once you get off them because they can see it's a hire car. Then they'll expect a bribe to let you go." She paused for effect. Not that old urban Mexican bent coppers myth I thought, but in anticipation of another twenty-five glorious years of marriage, I let it go.

We listened patiently as Amy went through what we could do in Mexico unmolested by the locals. There was Coco Bongo, "half disco, half Las Vegas show". Or the Pirate Ship with a real life Johnny Depp lookalike. Or we could swim with the dolphins. There were gold and silver packages or we could spend a whole day with the dolphins. When I explained the kind of things we would like to see Amy sighed. "Ah. History People," she said.

Now I may be a little thin-skinned, but does Thomson have a classroom at the back of Manchester Airport freight terminal where they teach their reps about the four kinds of tourists they are likely to encounter? "Families are your safest bet. Loads of money, demanding kids and shit scared of the locals. Young people are trouble. Give them nightclubs, water sports and cheap drink, then hope they get drunk and fight on someone else's watch. Married couples, mind, are good value. They've got money too and want to spend it. Tourist tat, shows. Easy. But History People. God save us from History People."

However, Amy did have something for us: day trips to the Mayan temples of Chichen Itza and Coba, where the pyramid is "the tallest in the Riviera Maya and they let you climb to the top." Bingo! In fact young Amy got quite enthused by it all. "The Mayans are still around," she said. "There are some here in the hotel. You'll see them for yourself. They're really short and have a funny shaped nose. Sort of hooked." Was she talking about the Mayans or the Munchkins?

But it's strange how things turn out because Amy's partner in crime, Raul Torres, a school teacher turned tour guide had a passion for the history and culture of his own people, the Mayans. And no, he didn't have a hooked nose. On our air-conditioned tour bus he'd given us a potted history of the Mayan people. "It was never an empire in the traditional sense," he said, as the teenager in the next seat plugged her earphones into her iPad. (Not part of a History Family obviously.) "Rather, it was a chain of city states stretching down from Tabasco across the Yucatán and into what we now call Belize, Guatemala and El Salvador." He talked us through their gods and religious rites and described Quetzalcoatl, the Mesoamerican deity who takes the form of a feathered serpent. Raul had difficulty describing the mythical beast.

"¿Como se dice?" he said in Spanish. "How do you say?" He

rolled up the left sleeve of his Thomson travel guide's polo shirt to reveal a coiled, feathered serpent on his upper arm. Raul was tattooed just like his ancestors had been and with the same deific symbol. Was he making a point about the continuity of culture? I didn't ask Jeff and his Californian wife sitting in front of me for their opinion. Nor their teenage daughter on my left whose headphones were by now emanating a tinny hissing sound.

The bus stopped and we made our way through the jungle to the pyramid temple of Coba. "These are called white roads," Raul told us, "because the passage of feet and animals has worn them down to the bare limestone. This road leads you in a straight line sixty-five kilometres to the main temple of Chichen Itza. That may be the bigger temple but this is the only one you can climb." We knew this already as Raul had made us sign an insurance disclaimer on the bus to allow us to climb the sacred mount. "Enjoy it while you can," he added. "I'll bet when your children come here it will all be cordoned off and made safe."

Helen grabbed my hand as I was about to bolt up the 142 steps to the altar at the top. This temple hadn't yet been 'restored' and the stones were uneven, weathered and pockmarked. "I'm feeling a bit dizzy," said Helen. She'd counted just twenty steps. I did the sympathetic husband thing. And then set off again on my own. These pyramids were the holiest of holies for the Mayans. Cities were laid out from them concentrically with the priests' and nobles' residences built nearest the centre. There was often a wall between them and the peasants. Today the jungle had reclaimed almost everything and the former city of 65,000 inhabitants had returned to a state of nature.

Apart from its size and shape the pyramid of Coba was rather unremarkable with no ornamentation to talk of. However, at the top as you looked steeply down you felt detached from the world, literally set apart. It was at an altar here that the Mayans sacrificed human beings to appease the god of creation. They believed that drops of the sun god existed in every single person. To ensure that the god continued to provide a bountiful harvest, and especially at the equinox, human hearts were torn out of living men and offered to him. It was an honour to die like this. The sons of the royalty were raised knowing that this would be their fate. The best military commanders too would be sacrificed. All of them apparently climbed the steps to the razor-sharp obsidian knife of the high priest willingly.

From the top of the pyramid you could sense the power these priests must have felt. High above the royal family, higher still than the people whose crops they were helping protect through blood, they held life in their hands. Above the altar there was nothing but the heavens. About them, a clear view of the whole known world. Masters of the universe.

In the shade of a tree I gave Helen some water. Raul came over. "Let me get you two a photo." I think my questioning on the walk through the jungle had made him like us. "Some people think the whole Mayan thing is vile and barbaric," he said. "But every culture has periods of murder and atrocity." He was talking to himself as much as he was to us. And of course he was right. Greek sieges, Roman attrition, the Crusades and two world wars. Europe had eaten itself on an alarmingly regular basis. We discussed belief and self-sacrifice. Hadn't we had the Spanish Inquisition where Jews, Moslems and anyone else suspected of impure thought would rather burn alive than recant their religious belief? And how about today's suicide bombers? Some things, countries, ideas, faith, are bigger than the individual, more important than the self. We still remember if not celebrate the Great War. Every person who goes to war is offering his or her life for a better tomorrow, one they may never see. And weren't we in Europe still burning witches long after the Mayan culture had been assimilated?

Raul snapped back into tour guide mode and led the party to a standing stone under a palm canopy. It depicted the king in ceremonial regalia, his head duly covered in the quetzal bird's plumage. Surrounding this were boxes of hieroglyphics.

"The Mayans had a sort of binary system for numbers," Raul told us. "A dot for one and a dash for five. Look! Here we can see the actual date the king had the stone carved. In our alphabet too we had more characters than you. Some of them are sounds, some pictures. And do you know we made a statement about mathematics and philosophy which the Romans never did? We knew of zero."

Jeff's daughter sucked hard on her Diet Coke, making a gurgling sound, and played with a tiny stray cat, her back turned firmly on class, but Raul was in his stride. "We know that the Mayans mapped the movement of the moon, the sun, Venus. They predicted the whole alignment of the planets in 2012. That's where their calendar stopped. Some nutty Californians decided that it signified the end of the world and thousands came to Coba for the midsummer solstice. I don't know whether they expected to die here." Raul laughed. Our very own Californian family looked bemused. "It was the best advertisement this place ever had," said Raul triumphantly.

We drove just down the road from the temple to a 'typical' Mayan village. It was a pretty uninspiring mix of single-storey adobe shacks and breeze-block sheds on the edge of Lake Coba. "Look to your left," said Raul and fifty-two heads swivelled left. "See that school? It's an indigenous school. In the Yucatán province all high school children must now learn Mayan. I came from a Mayan family but Spanish is my first language. My parents wouldn't speak to me in Mayan. To get on you needed to speak Spanish." Helen and I nodded to each other knowingly.

There are in fact dozens of Mayan languages spoken by some six million people across Central America. Raul's family are some of the 800,000 people who speak Yucatec Maya, known simply as Maya. It is still a common first language in the villages but the more contact there is with Spanish-speaking towns and tourists, the more diluted it becomes. As Raul put it, "Mayan maybe at home, Spanish mostly in school and English for the tourists."

Señora Ramona welcomed us into her cluster of huts. One half-whitewashed block with a corrugated roof stood out from the other more traditional buildings. After a bad hurricane in 2005 this whole area had been devastated. So the Mexican government decided to raise a storm-resistant communal stone building in every Mayan village. But this one stands empty. The traditional wood and palm-leaf buildings are built to a Mayan family's personal specifications. The design will change depending on that family's height, what purpose it will serve and how long they are likely to need it. This new 'village hall' from the government was not designed that way at all. It was just built. Looking at the unused breeze-block gift from the central government Raul shrugged.

Ramona showed us around the 'sleeping house'. There was not a stick of furniture, only hammocks thrown between the wooden poles which held the roof up. The family's clothes were kept in plastic bags tied to a line slung across the back of the room. Helen sat with the mistress of the house and watched her pat tortillas down on a broad stone and cook them on an open fire. We nibbled politely scooping some spicy salsa into the dough. Back home this would be called a living museum. Here it's classed as cultural tourism. As I handed the fruit I had brought for the children to the Señora I felt rather undignified. I wondered how Ramona felt.

In another hut, the workshop, there was an ancient hand-driven Singer sewing machine. This is where Ramona makes and embroiders the *huipiles*, the traditional Mayan white smocks she sells to tourists. The necks have an intricate and richly coloured yoke of flowers and leaves. Outside the workshop I noticed a satellite dish on one roof. Importing Spanish football, wrestling and *telenovelas*.

Ramona's children leave the village every day to work in the tourism business, serving in hotels and bars or nick-nack shops. Her grandchildren ran barefoot amongst us and offered us flowers as we left. Some of our group stuffed dollar bills into their hands even though we'd been told not to.

We left the main Cancún highway and its tourist buses and headed down a dirt road which came to an abrupt stop. Under a cool canopy of trees we took a short walk over the crumbling stones to a small clearing in the jungle. A man in white trousers with a mop of black hair was fanning a smoking crucible. The smoke had a delicate perfume but was in no way sweet. "It's a bit like the incense in church," I said to Helen. This we were told was the Mayan shaman and he was about to bless us. Helen is a good Catholic and I thought that she might have baulked at being part of this pagan right. Maybe it was the incense but she was first in line to hear the strange incantation and receive the smoke the shaman flicked over her bowed head with a fan of green reeds. Helen clutched a fistful of smoke tight to her chest as she'd been told and made a prayer. It was like making a wish over a shooting star. I suppose superstition is the same in every culture.

As the ceremony ended Raul nodded approvingly. "It's been twenty years since I attended a proper Mayan ceremony. They last from dawn to dusk," he said before thanking the shaman, in Spanish.

A short walk through the wood brought us out at an expansive souvenir shop. We were fed, not unwillingly, a glass of local tequila. The owner saw me examine a black obsidian dagger. My mind went back to the hideous sacrificial ceremonies Raul had described unflinchingly.

"This stone's so hard that we have to use a diamond drill to cut it these days," said the shopkeeper.

"Do you get it from around here?" I asked.

"Oh no. This stuff comes from central Mexico. The Mayans traded all sorts of stuff, fruit, cloth and whatever, to get the obsidian. See that jade?" He pointed to a facsimile of a royal funeral mask. "That comes from south of here. Our people travelled far and wide around the waters of the Yucatán peninsula. Inland too." He didn't seem to be pitching for a sale. "All this work is done locally, young lads and women using traditional methods," he added as if to offer some slim line of continuity between today and the golden age of Mayan civilisation.

According to Raul the Mayans were never conquered. The glory days of the old empire lasted more than 600 years between 320 and 990 AD. They founded major cities in Tikal, Coba and of course the great Chichen Itza. They expressed themselves through fine art and perfected writing. No-one knows why but by the end of the tenth century they had abandoned the great cities. After their own Dark Ages the Mayans regrouped and merged with the incoming Toltecs under the guidance of Quetzalcoatl who was later deified as Kukulkan. When the Spanish reached the peninsula in the early 1600s they were met with considerable opposition and it took almost half a century to tame the Mayans. Despite repression, Mexican independence and a string of revolutions they have survived.

On the way home Raul talked to us about his family. His son Armando was studying business and his twenty-one-year-old daughter Jessica was already working in hotel administration. Yes, they both had some Mayan words and could hold a rudimentary conversation in the language. In the country, his cousins held onto some aspects of the old ways. They used the healing qualities of obsidian rock, could still blend traditional medicines and sometimes consulted the shaman. Raul said the Mayan language too was undergoing a bit of a revival.

'Cultural' tourism is relatively new to Mexico. Our dollars are supposed to support the rural communities and help keep the language alive. There are 600 ancient Mayan sites but only sixty have been excavated, and then only partly. The jungle is being cut down to reveal the hidden architectural and artistic treasures of the golden age. We come to see that culture, meet the last of the Mayan people and take comfort in being told we are somehow helping them, that we do good by doing so.

Over two bulbous glasses of piña colada at the poolside bar of the sumptuous Riu Palace hotel, Helen and I discussed our day out.

"Do you think we're part of the problem?" she said, opening and closing the blue-and-pink mini-parasol of her drink.

"You know. We come here, lie on a white beach for a few days. Then out we go, snap the history and culture with our digital cameras and while we're there we throw the peasants a few pesos to salve our conscience."

"It was fruit for the children," I said defensively, "and anyway why should we feel guilty?"

"Maybe, but the holiday industry is a twin-edged sword, isn't it? God, we know that from the way Abersoch and the Llŷn peninsula has become a playground for the English. House prices there have driven the locals out and don't start me on the loss of the Welsh language."

We ordered another piña colada. *"Gracias,"* said Helen to the young man with the funny shaped nose.

"I mean they've all got to speak Spanish to work here, haven't they?"

Perhaps Raul was right about 'catching it now'. Like they are doing with the pyramids themselves, one day soon they will build a wall around the very last Mayan. We will board an air-conditioned bus to his village, sling him twenty dollars and gawp at him fanning incense while mumbling away in a lost language only he understands. And all this because of us. History People, eh?

The last day of the revolution

August 2014

THE FLAMES OF yesterday's riot may have been put out, most of the wreckage cleared away, but the remains of the burning tyres were still there, sticking to our feet. We trod gingerly across Khreshchatyk Street and on down to Maidan Square in the centre of Kyiv. The blackened toffee of the tarmac was littered with rocks and splintered wood. The air was rank with the smell of burned rubber. A young man in tattered combat trousers and military boots walked briskly past us. He was carrying a cosh, too short to be a baseball bat, but probably all the more useful because of that. He was topless, had a toned body and his head was shaved except for a long straggly pony tail which sort of quiffed forward into his eyes. "They cut it like that deliberately," said Chester knowingly. "It's how the Ukrainian fighters used to wear it centuries ago. Some kind of tribute, I guess."

Twelve hours earlier this place had been mayhem as the Maidan protest dragged on. The barricades had been set alight when the police once again tried to clear the area and bring some semblance of normality to the Ukrainian capital. Chester had arrived the day before his mum and dad and was glad to have seen the dying flames of a revolution. A real revolution. Helen was not so keen and stuck close to me. But I had done her wedding anniversary holiday, now it was time for her to do mine.

"Of course, Dad, you missed the action," said Chester triumphantly. Now he was giving us a guided tour of the square and was rather proud that he'd got one over on the old man. "This morning they were stockpiling firebombs behind that barricade. That armoured car thing was in flames. There was no way through over there either," he said pointing to the piles of furniture and rubbish on the hill leading up to the government buildings. It was on this hill, Instytus'ka, that many of the protestors had been shot by government snipers in February. Today, men, and some women, were again battling, this time for the right to remain in this central part of Kyiv. Even the spelling of the capital city's name is contentious. Kiev is the less favoured Russian translation. Kyiv is the Ukrainian way, used by the national poet, Taras Shevchenko, and in all official government documentation since 1995.

Those who were still in the Maidan had left their studies and jobs to fight for a fairer, more honest Ukraine. They'd been there since the protests started and now their jobs and college courses were lost to them. This struggle had become their lives. To what could they return? When the opposition leader Yulia Tymoshenko was released from prison there was talk of an amnesty for the protestors. "Go home and get your lives back on track," they'd been told. "Let us sort this out." But they didn't believe her and feared that if they did leave there would be an early morning knock on the door, unknown dark forces on their doorstep and they would simply disappear. Echoes of the KGB days of the USSR perhaps, but it was a genuine fear.

The struggle for the Maidan started in December 2013 and had been going on for nine months. All through the hard winter there were street protests and riots with many of the fighters camping in and around the square itself. The dreaded Berkut, the 'special' police, would attack. The people would fight back with whatever they had to hand. Over the weeks and months the protests escalated. There was an explosion and an exchange of gunfire. Then on Tuesday, the 18th of February, at least twenty-six people from both sides were killed. They called a truce on the Wednesday but the next day fifty people were killed on Instytus'ka. Finally and having opened fire on his own people the hated president, Viktor Yanukovych, fled to Russia. Of course the shockwaves of that day are still being felt. The Russians annexed the Crimea. What we were told were pro-Russian fighters took control of Donetsk and Lugansk on the border and Ukraine teetered on the verge of civil war.

Chester was enthused. At last here was a real bottom-up revolution, and he was in the thick of it. We were unsure about who was right and who was wrong. After all, the government which was overthrown had been democratically elected, hadn't it? What was not in dispute though was that the people had raised barricades, taken on the state and overthrown the president. Tonight though the Maidan was the most welcoming of battlegrounds. Khaki military tents were surrounded by garish open-air bars with jolly red plastic chairs and tables. We sat and sipped a beer as a young man came out of the tent flap and sat on a low stool. A woman appeared with a bowl and a rag and proceeded to tend to his cut eye. We were not unwelcome here, we were simply ignored. For the diehard activists it was business as usual.

A lorry pulled up behind us and parked in front of the central post office. Half-a-dozen men, some wearing ski masks, jumped down and started unloading tyres, stacking them across the steps to block the entrance to the metro station. Riot police had launched attacks from the subway itself and those remaining in the Maidan were not going to be caught out. Bottles and a jerry can presumably full of petrol were neatly lined up. Another man casually stacked the grey bricks which used to be a pavement into rows on the walls of the underground passage. There was no 'authority' to be seen, no police, no military. Helen squeezed my hand in a silent plea to get out of here. Yet there was a calmness about it all, as if the rioters were just going through their evening routine. The Maidan may have been lawless but at the same time it was totally peaceful. We had walked into a bizarre form of 'revo-tourism.' "Hello. Why don't you buy a pint, sit down and relax while you watch us gear up for tomorrow's riot? No really, we do this every night."

An upright piano painted in the national colours of blue and yellow had been dumped outside the post office and a man with long shaggy hair was playing a wistful piece of music. But what none of us knew was that tonight was to be the very last night of this peculiar Ukrainian prom. The people of Kyiv, who had mostly supported the protests, felt it had all come to a natural end. They now wanted their city back.

The next morning the mayor, world heavyweight boxing champion turned politician Vitali Klitschko, gathered a hundred or so volunteers, walked into the centre of town and started to clear the square. They filled lorries with the wrecked furniture, planks and the ubiquitous tyres and finally, gently, sent everyone home. They were backed up by the Kyiv-1 Battalion, a group of volunteer soldiers who had recently seen action in the Crimea and in the east of the country. These guys had started their new military careers on the barricades of the Maidan. "It gives them a moral edge, doesn't it?" said Chester. "You know. They probably just said to this lot here, 'OK guys, you wanna fight for the motherland? Then come join us on the frontline in Crimea or in Donetsk. We'll show you real war.'"

That afternoon we retraced our steps and walked from the post office across the square to meet John Barrow, a teacher who had lived in Ukraine for seven years. The change was quite remarkable. Gone were the barricades, the tents and the ragged protestors. There was a sense of normality about the place, as if the city were breathing a collective sigh of relief. As we tried to dodge the cars now filling Khreshchatyk Street, the main road to the Maidan, a policeman waved his baton at us gesturing for us to use the crossing. City life was back to normal. We did as we were told, walking past the massive iron Christmas tree which was covered in pictures, flags and posters. Christmas was nine months ago but this metal skeleton with its home-made cloth coverings had become a shrine to all those who had fallen in the conflict.

On the brow of Instytus'ka John stopped us. "This is the way I walk to work," he said. "I was caught up in that first attack in February and saw two corpses just there outside the metro station." John filmed what he saw. "There was a man lying on the ground, a woman to the right, on the barricade itself. I actually took this film as evidence of the deaths, as the government was in full denial mode at the time. Both protestors apparently died from blows, not gunshot. I checked the woman for vital signs but it was no good."

The Euromaidanpr Facebook page describes the incident John witnessed: "Antonina Dvorianets was at Maidan for better future of her children and grandchildren. The day she died she took part in peaceful picketing of the Rada (Ukrainian parliament) to make the people's will known to MPs. She was beaten dead with truncheons by riot police." Antonina was sixty-two, retired and a former 'liquidator' who had risked her life making safe the Chernobyl nuclear disaster site, seventy miles from Kiyv.

"I actually tried to contact her family," said John. "I'd read that they knew nothing of the circumstances of her death. I was later told that the body was only released to them on condition they sign a fraudulent coroner's report stating she'd died of natural causes – a heart attack."

Nearby was a small roadside shrine where a home-made riot shield lay against a tree upon which the picture of a young man was nailed. There were bright orange construction hats on the ground at the base of the tree, makeshift helmets which had been used in the heat of the battle.

We looked up at the massive red-and-black flag tied across the bridge above Instytus'ka. Flags had been a big deal during the protests. The Maidan Christmas tree, the protestors' tents and the buildings along the broad avenue all flew the flags of different countries. The previous night we'd been amazed to see the Welsh Dragon shivering from a pole atop one barricade.

"Львівска брама," said John. "It's Lviv Bridge. The red and black stand for blood and soil."

"Blood and soil?" I said. "Doesn't that have a certain fascist ring to it?"

"No," said John adamantly. "The word 'fascist' has been abused here by all sides. They throw it at each other all too freely but what does it actually mean? The people in control now were all elected under the old system so you could argue that they're all tainted. What they did here was a popular change of power. Now they want the system itself changed."

We had also seen a flag stating "Stop Russian Fascism". Over lunch we discussed the historical context of fascism in Eastern Europe and the rights and wrongs of popular revolt. Was removing a democratically elected president, however bad, through street demonstrations and violence itself a fascist act? How about annexing the Crimea without a ballot? I was confused. We were all confused.

John tried to explain. "It's too easy to see this as a fight between pro-European and pro-Russian factions. It's more complex than that." Some want to change the electoral process and bring in some form of PR. The protestors want more than just a change of personnel at the top. "You see," said John, "Ukraine has become a post-Soviet kleptocracy. Cronyism is rife, the people at the top are unaccountable and the whole rotten system has been enforced by a nasty security apparatus. Those people you saw yesterday, they're fighting for ownership of the Maidan, the legacy of the protests, and of course a real change of political culture."

We looked around us at the debris of a popular revolt. Council workers had started cutting the grass verges and were re-laying the grey block pavement. "If you want to portray it as East versus West then fine," said John. "But it was, is, more fundamental than that. It's about how you want society organised and run. Really basic stuff."

Overnight thirteen men had been killed in Donetsk as Ukrainian government forces battled what we were told were pro-Russian rebels. Shells had been fired into residential neighbourhoods. Why, I did not know. East, West, EU, Russia. Who knows what they were thinking? Maybe the people in the east were having their own Maidan moment, a jerky realignment of a wronged history. I just hoped it wouldn't last as long as this one in Kyiv had.

Turn right at the camel

April 2015

"JUST TURN RIGHT at the camel," they said. "You'll find the Bedouin camp there. It's somewhere off Route One between Jerusalem and Jericho." And indeed a few miles along the smooth four-lane tarmac highway at the junction sat the camel. The road signs had been telling us our increasing depth below sea level as we sped towards the Dead Sea, the lowest place on earth. Halfway down, the camel sat, shiny silver ornamental droplets shimmering on his red cloth saddle-cum-overcoat. His master was hoping for a tourist to pull over and have his picture taken for a couple of shekels, but we turned right as we'd been told.

Wales were playing football in Haifa but most of the supporters had heeded the over cautious advice and stayed on the beach in Tel Aviv. Chester and I wanted to get a balanced picture of Israel and had heard that because of their lifestyle the Bedouins were particularly vulnerable under the Israeli occupation. Meeting some of them seemed like a good place to start.

Leaving the city of Jerusalem and its suburbs and passing through the military checkpoint you almost flow through a series of massive bald white bumps, oversized bulls' noses of rock ripped open by deep ridges and ravines. There was a thin covering of green to break up the barren landscape. It was early spring but lush this land was not. "It's almost biblical, isn't it?" I said to Chester with a childish grin. He humoured me. Every so often, lone teenagers in jumpers stood watching their flock of shaggy, cloth-eared sheep. The luckier ones sat on the back of a donkey and wielded a stick. We turned sharply off the tarmac, waved at the camel owner, negotiated a dried out river bed, went up and round and round again through the rocks until we reached the Bedouin camp.

Wadi al Qteyf or Sateh al Bahar, which means Sea Level, is a ramshackle collection of about a dozen containers, the kind of things you see on a dockside or in a railway siding. Some had a sheet of plastic or a black tarpaulin fixed with rope and tyres as an awning. Sheep and goats were penned tightly into corrals, mashing up the earth beneath their feet. There's no running water here, no mains electricity and the builder style bogs and the portable accommodation blocks have all been donated by the European Union. It says so with a nice logo on the side of each one.

Our friend from home was living in Jerusalem and said he knew just the person to show us around. Nicola Harrison works for the United Nations and is an expert on Palestinian Bedouins. She's a fluent Arabic speaker and seemed to know anyone who's anyone in Wadi al Qteyf. I asked Nicola how many people live in isolated communities like this.

"Difficult to say," she said. "The Palestinian Authority doesn't single them out but we estimate there are around 30,000 Bedouins living in Area C."

Area C is the sixty per cent of Palestinian land which is under full Israeli military and administrative control as set out in the Oslo Accords which outlined who ran which parts of the West Bank. The Accords envisioned that Area C would be a temporary measure and that by 1990 it was to be incrementally handed over to Palestinian control. This never happened.

We got down from the 4x4, took our shoes off and sat cross-legged on cushions on the floor of the largest container in the camp. One side was open to the elements and we were sheltered by a large plastic cover held up with wooden poles. It kept the sun off us and flapped gently above our heads. The floor was covered in weathered overlapping patterned carpets.

As the crow flies we were very near the highway but it was quiet here, serene.

Against the opposite wall sat Khalil, father and grandfather of the Hammadeen family, part of the Jahalin tribe. He cut an imposing figure in a simple, dark grey, ankle-length *tob* (robe), his head covered in a brilliant white *kufiya*. His face was weathered, he had a well-kept grey-white beard and he constantly fingered a string of yellow beads in his right hand. We sat together nervously adjusting our legs and feet under us, trying to get comfortable. Despite there being a massive settee behind him, Khalil sat impassively on a thin mattress right in front of it. It was difficult to say what age he was. I'm not sure he understood much of what was going on but the younger people and we in turn showed deference towards him.

Khalil welcomed us and gestured to one of his grandsons. The young man hurried about pouring strong coffee from an outsized silver pot into small, patterned glasses. It looked ceremonial. Maybe it was. The coffee was flavoured with cardamom which was so bitter my mouth instantly dried up.

Khalil's son Jamil was smart, polite and spoke very good English. Unlike his dad he was dressed in jeans, polo shirt and a black leather jacket. He was unusual in that he'd gone to college and had studied business in the city of Hebron. (Never mind areas A, B and C, in Hebron the city itself is divided into Jewish and Arab sectors delineated by concrete blocks, barbed wire and guard towers.) Jamil was trying to put into practice some of what he'd learned in college and was taking small, tentative steps to diversify the family's livelihood with a bit of 'Bedouin tourism'.

On our way up through the camp we'd seen a group of Israelis eating lunch in a hut under the shade of corrugated sheets. They worked for a human rights group and had chosen to spend their work's away day learning a little about Arab culture. That morning they had walked over the bald hills hearing about their near neighbours' very different way of life. Just by being here the Israelis were making a statement to their countrymen. By inviting them into his family home so was Jamil.

Nicola translated for us. "All these camps are considered illegal under Israeli military law and the Hammadeens live in fear that the Israeli Defence Force will come in one night and just bulldoze all this down."

Jamil told us about how they have traditionally made a living on this inhospitable land. "We graze our animals on what grass we can find but the main meat market is in Israel proper. Going through the checkpoints and the hassle we get makes it difficult for us to keep going."

"Why do they want to live like this?" I whispered to Nicola.

"It's all about their traditions," she said. "They'd like to develop their communities here but they're living under the constant threat of eviction. It's just not easy."

Years ago of course, the Bedouin lived in tents made out of woven goat or camel hair. It has a unique ability to keep them cool in the summer and warm in the colder months. They roamed around pretty much where they chose. Today the lads here go and work wherever they can in the towns to make ends meet, building work or doing odd jobs.

"The Palestinian Bedouins live in extended family groups and traditionally the women are not supposed to be seen by any Bedouin men other than a blood relative," Nicola told us. Chester and I wriggled a bit. It was true. We hadn't seen a single Bedouin woman.

"Sounds like enslavement to me," Chester said under his breath. "Are we supporting a return to the Middle Ages? We wouldn't accept that at home, would we?" It was a fair point but one we did not pursue.

The Israelis are building a new town to 'house' the Bedouins just a few miles north of Wadi al Qteyf. But merging tens of individual communities into one town would isolate the women in their homes. They would not be able to move around freely as they can now in their own family communities. Urban living doesn't fit with this unique family group structure. If they were all moved into a town there would be no place to graze the animals. Khalil and his family would become urbanised. In effect they would cease to be Bedouins. Maybe that's the point.

Nicola later explained a bit more about the role of women to us. "Women are cherished in Bedouin society. They're vital really. They're the ones who make and trade all the milk products. Women can travel alone and within the community they're in full control of the private domain, whilst men manage the public domain."

The formalities over and our respects duly paid to the father of the family, Jamil led us down to the community kindergarten, another shed with no door. In place of a whiteboard there was a piece of cardboard pinned to the front wall with some childish scribbles in chalk on it. Jamil pointed up to the coarse wooden beams which held the roof up. "That's the fruit of our first profits from the project," he beamed. I doubt it had cost more than £100.

Most of the children here will go to school at some point. Jamil has the keys to the community's only car and drives a small group of them the ten or so miles to school in Jericho most mornings. But there is no formal pre-school education and there are high levels of illiteracy among the Bedouins. This kindergarten is one of only a handful of self-help schools across the Judean desert.

The Israeli authorities and the active settler pressure groups in particular don't like the Hammadeen community. It stands in the way of their eastward march towards the river Jordan. Just a couple of miles away, hidden for the time being by the mountains, lies Ma'ale Adumim, home to more than 40,000 Jewish settlers. Its two fingers of development dig deep into Palestine. Over the next hill is a massive industrial estate, where dozens of high tech and manufacturing companies have set up. And not far away again are the settlements of Nofei Prat and Kfar Adumim. The Israeli Housing minister used to live here. In an illegal settlement. This was the man who made decisions about when and how Palestinians could build on land in Area C.

All the Israeli settlements are illegal according to the United Nations. Only the outposts to the existing settlements are illegal according to Israeli law. Transport containers, just like the ones the Bedouins live in are dropped off the back of a truck a few hundred yards from the 'legal' Israeli settlement. Ultra-Zionists move into the containers with sleeping bags and make do. In a couple of years the containers are linked to the main settlement by roads, electricity and water. The illegal becomes legal and hey presto the land is now under full Jewish Israeli control.

In stark contrast to the bright white Israeli tower blocks on the hills the ramshackle permanent impermanent Bedouin hamlets are under constant threat. None has a building permit. Many have been bulldozed and the residents forcibly resettled. Not far from here is an army base on top of a hill. "There's a bed and breakfast for the animals up there," we'd been told. Eh?

"If the Bedouins' animals stray anywhere near the Israeli settlements the army will confiscate the sheep or goats and take them to the base. Fines have to be paid to have the animals returned and a daily fee is charged for food during their incarceration. It's true," said Nicola without a smile.

Further along the mountain from Wadi al Qteyf there is an armoured police station. This is the first building in yet another Israeli settlement. The noose is tightening around every Palestinian community in Area C but because of their lifestyle and the fact that they live in small, semi nomadic groups, the Bedouins are more vulnerable and defenceless than those living in towns and villages.

The Bedouins are Arab and are therefore seen as 'a security threat.' The S word, 'Security', gives the state, the Israeli Defence Force and the Housing minister himself every justification to demolish homes, displace families and force them to change their way of life. The United Nations says there are 7,000

Bedouins living in the West Bank who are at risk of immediate forced 'relocation'. Ninety per cent of them depend on herding as their primary source of income. For how much longer we just don't know.

There is a vile inevitability to it all. The Israelis want to drive the Palestinians out of large areas of their homeland and inch by inch they are doing just that. But Jamil Hammadeen is young, has hope and has great plans for his community now that his 'eco-tourism' project is taking off.

"We're going to have a Bedouin museum right here in Wadi al Qteyf," he said with pride. There was no defiance in his voice and I wondered whether he was in denial of what was happening all around him.

"We're collecting objects and stuff from all the people here."

Jamil had asked every family to contribute something to the museum to record their history and he had already received his first exhibit. It was an old wedding blanket in which the newly married couple are traditionally wrapped as they stand in the middle of their families and friends. The ceremony represents the kinship and protection the extended family will give the newlyweds and their offspring.

"We'll show them all in our museum," said Jamil excitedly. "People will come from Jerusalem and see our history and we'll help them to understand our Bedouin culture."

I would like to think that the museum will provide a record of a living culture but I have my doubts. My last question to Jamil was meant to demonstrate some moral support for his family's situation.

"Do you think your grandchildren will be born here and live like you and your father do?"

His reply was not long and it was not in English but I understood it. *"Inshallah,"* said Jamil, *"Inshallah."*

***

The Peace Wall which divides Israel and most of the Palestinian Territories is the most obvious and brutal manifestation of the troubles here. Chester and I had travelled to Bethlehem where the wall abuts the Little Town. A street ends, and there it is. I photographed the spray-painted image of Leila Khaled who became the exotic 1960s poster girl of the Palestinian cause. She was the archetypal freedom fighter who was famously photographed wrapped in a *kufiya* as she hugged her AK-47. I told Chester how her hijacking of an aeroplane was one of my earliest television memories. The images of jumbo jets being blown up in the desert, of a just cause, of young people bearing arms were heady to a child living in a small town in Harold Wilson's Britain. The pictures then were in black and white and I guess so were the politics of it all. Chester pointed to the graffiti next to Khaled's image. It read CTRL-ALT-DELETE, a cheeky modern reference to the long-term impact of Israeli occupation. The wall may be the most obvious symbol of the division but to feel its real heat you need to travel a few more miles south, to Hebron.

Jamal sat on a low stool in his tiny drapery shop in the heart of the Old City. His was an Aladdin's cave of kaleidoscopic colours and patterns. Carpets were piled high against the walls. Scarves, shawls and blankets hung from the ceiling. Gold and red threads were weaved into black and blue and green cottons in traditional Palestinian patterns. Jamal explained to us that the new fibres aren't as good as the old. "The new ones, they lose their colour too quickly. One wash and they fade," he said. But business in the bazaar was bad. Very bad. Because Jamal's shop is literally the end of the road. Israeli settlers have annexed this side of town and closed Shuhada Street. His and his neighbours' shops have become a front line beyond which no Palestinian can easily go.

"No-one comes here any more," Jamal said wistfully. "They all shop in the new town. You can understand it I suppose." He rose slowly and gestured me towards the entrance of the shop. "Come over here. Look!" Jamal pointed upwards to where the sunlight pierced the alleyway. A few feet above our heads a heavy wire mesh cut off the shops from the residential floors above. Here and there blue-and-white Israeli flags fluttered from windows and roofs. Jamal turned a pashmina over with his weather-beaten hand. It was stained with what looked like egg. "They throw all sorts down at us," he said. I looked up and saw plastic bottles, lumps of concrete and broken glass lying on the wire above. "Sometimes they throw other things down. Dirty water, other fluids. You know what I mean?"

Hebron lies twenty miles south of Jerusalem in the Palestinian Territories. You have to cross through the 'Peace' Wall and navigate an Israeli checkpoint to get here. The journey has the whiff of the Cold War about it, complete with a twenty-first-century Berlin Wall, tortured graffiti and potentially trigger-happy border guards. And just as we did with its German communist counterpart when that finally came down, sometime in the future we will ask, "A wall to divide society? How on earth could we have let this happen?"

Jamal was fifty-two but he looked older. He had studied metallurgy in Manchester, loved his time in England and despite his commitment to the Palestinian cause is a bit of an Anglophile. His father was what he called a 'tribal chief' and a local politician. As they passed his shop everyone greeted Jamal warmly and with respect. When his father died Jamal upped sticks and returned to Hebron to run the family business.

We walked together some fifty yards into a small square where a few scrawny chickens were being kept in cages. One or two ran loose in the street. "This used to be the meat and poultry market," said Jamal. "See. It's blocked off just there. We only keep a few birds here now. Storage." Behind the concrete slabs which abruptly blocked off the alley and surrounded by barbed wire there was a three-storey synagogue. The whole front of the building had been painted with a giant Jewish candlestick. "That used to be our school," said Jamal. "The settlers stole it and built up and up."

As we were walking through the old town to meet Jamal,

Chester had bought a wristband from a child who had harangued us in Arabic. The band was made out of beads in the colours of the Palestinian flag – green, red, white and black. It was Chester's small act of solidarity. He was chuffed with his purchase but I wondered whether it would get us into trouble with the Israelis.

Home to the Tomb of the Patriarchs, Abraham, Isaac and Jacob, Hebron is the oldest Jewish city. It is also one of the four holy cities of Islam but is divided along religious lines. History is pretty raw here. In 1994 an American-born Jewish settler called Baruch Goldstein opened fire on unarmed Palestinian Muslims praying inside the mosque during Ramadan. Twenty-nine worshippers were killed and 125 wounded. The attack only ended after Goldstein had expended his ammunition. He was overcome and beaten to death by survivors.

Following the 1995 Oslo Agreement, Hebron was split into two sectors: 170,000 Palestinians live under Palestinian Authority control in the romantically named H1, alongside but not among the 600 Israelis who live in the supposedly mixed community of H2. The Israeli Defence Force may not enter H1 unless under Palestinian escort and Palestinians cannot approach settler areas without special permits. The Jewish settlement is considered to be illegal by the international community. And also by Jamal.

The name Hebron in both Hebrew and Arabic means 'the friend'. The Old City hadn't changed for centuries prior to the Israeli occupation. It's a maze of narrow, winding streets, flat-roofed stone houses and old bazaars. Sandaled feet have smoothed the white floors of the market until they almost shine. It's all rather romantic, if you don't look up.

In 1994 however, after the shooting, the main market area, Al-Shuhada Street, was closed by military order to Palestinian vehicles and pedestrians. Concrete barricades, razor wire and heavy metal doors have created a not so 'green' line splitting the Old City in two. Shuhada Street was supposed to have reopened, but since the Second Intifada in 2000 it has been even more firmly closed to Palestinians. Jamal's problem is that although he lives in H1 his shop backs right onto Shuhada Street. The formerly bustling economy has been badly hit. Half the shops here have closed and according to a study by the International Committee of the Red Cross in 2009, seventy-seven per cent of the Palestinians in Hebron's Old City live below the poverty line. "Go see it for yourself," said Jamal. "Shuhada Street's empty. Totally empty. They've stolen our homes and our livelihoods. Of course I can't take you there. You'll have to go by yourself through the checkpoint."

In the shadow of the Ibrahimi Mosque where the massacre had taken place the IDF guards looked bored. Chester and I were something of a novelty. The young soldier smiled. "What religion are you?" he said. Oh shit. Had he seen Chester's wristband? Thankfully not. I told him I was an atheist. He looked nonplussed. At the time I thought this was a clever reply, perhaps giving him pause for thought on religious bigotry and sectarianism. But it was a feeble attempt on my own part to make sense of it all, by telling him, myself, that religion itself may be the problem. The young guard checked our passports and waved us through.

The bustle of the teashops and cafes behind the mosque subsided as we walked almost reverentially along the deserted Shuhada Street. Chester broke the silence. "Jamal was right," he said. "It's a ghost town." There were no cars, no people, no business. Weeds grew along the kerbside. The metal shutters of the shop fronts had all been welded shut. Words in Arabic script were carved into the capping stones above the entrances but on every one of the hard, metal doors below, the Star of David had been sprayed. I had been told, but did not see it for myself, that at the top of the street the graffiti read "Gas the Arabs".

We rounded the corner to the back of Jamal's old school. Bikes were piled high near the doorway and I could hear the children inside. The old stone building was now a school and a synagogue and had been extended in modern materials, complete with uPVC doors and windows. It was guarded by an IDF watchtower below which there was a sign. It read, "These buildings were constructed on land purchased by the Hebron Jewish community in 1807. This land was stolen by Arabs following the murder of 67 Hebron Jews in 1929." Rights and wrongs. Tit for tat killings. How far back in history do we want to go?

We walked back through the checkpoint and into the souk with a sense of sadness, hopelessness even. Jamal though looked slightly smug. "I told you so," he said softly, sensing our shock. "They are trying to grind us down. Get rid of us." His eyes moved away from mine as if he were speaking to himself. "But they will never move me out. Never. Until I die."

***

Two orthodox Jews wearing furry, outsized pillbox hats disappeared into a side alley as we turned into St George's Street. Darkness had fallen over Jerusalem and it was now the Shabbat, the holy night and day when no work is to be done. The men had been to the Western Wall to offer their prayers and were walking home to break bread with their families. Our outsized black Ford swung onto the pavement and parked outside the United Nations compound. It was the last Friday of the month and time for the ex-pat and diplomatic community to let their hair down and party.

The UN's reception area had been turned into a disco and the sounds of Britpop and techno boomed from the wide open double doors. In 1948 this handsome former Arab town house had been the home of the Mixed Armistice Commission. More than fifty years on, though in a different guise, the monitors were still here.

Down the entrance steps and into the softly lit garden, diplomats, aid workers and hangers-on like Chester and I mingled over slippery bottles of German beer and lukewarm white wine. Some were 'working the room' in search of a tiny diplomatic breakthrough which might pierce Israeli intransigence and offer a crumb of hope for the Palestinians. On the other hand they may have been plotting their next career move or their rivals' downfall, poisoning the ear of the station boss with tales of incompetence or worse.

We'd been told not to let on to N-'s boss that she was going for a promotion outside the organisation. She was working with refugees on the West Bank and had recently been tear gassed by the Israeli Defence Force outside Bethlehem simply for being there and asking awkward questions. "We got an apology that time," she said, "but it isn't always that easy." The Israelis don't like the United Nations' presence here. They say there are no refugees, that all those people crammed into camps and pushed into the desert went there of their own volition in 1948. Move on, nothing to see. That there was such a sizeable crowd of humanitarian workers, observers and international aiders still here suggested otherwise.

Chester was by now a student of politics and genned-up on all things conflict from his beloved Balkans to South East Asia. This was his introduction to the social side of international diplomacy and we pressed the flesh with the best of them. R- was a big noise in humanitarian affairs. He said he was Sri Lankan though he was educated 'south of Oxford' he said vaguely. He spoke like a true English gent without a hint of an accent. "I haven't been back to Sri Lanka for, ooh, twenty years or more," he said. He was one of that band of homeless internationalists who are always on the move, stopping off somewhere and doing good for a year or two before moving on to a new country, a new challenge.

Kylie's 'Can't Get You Out of My Head' pumped through the night air followed by Oasis's 'Roll With It'. Despite there being a rainbow of nations represented here, English was the lingua franca and most of the partygoers were British or American. Though it was just a stone's throw from here, Jerusalem's Old Town, with its history and conflict, seemed another world. Perhaps the United Nations should be renamed the United

Western Nations, its mission as international peacekeeper changed to 'cultural colonialist' and Kylie installed as secretary general.

Now diplomats come in all shapes and sizes. A- was our very own 'Counsel for Palestine'.

"No ambassador, you see, as they're not really a country. Rather awkward isn't it?" he said in a thick Glaswegian accent, and laughed.

Chester shot me a look which said 'inappropriate'. I blinked my agreement at him. A burly Scot, A- wore a chain around his neck cradling an outsized pendant which bounced a little under his patterned, open-necked shirt. This was hardly the crisp linen-suited ambassador I had expected. But then there can't be an ambassador to Palestine, as A- had said, because it doesn't exist.

He was very keen to remind us that he came from Maryhill in Glasgow. "Where they filmed *Taggart*," he said as if we hadn't already noted his working-class credentials. "My predecessor was very different from me. Very English, very old fashioned. He couldn't even master e-mail."

When A- drew breath, which wasn't often, our host M- whispered to me hurriedly. "His predecessor may have been a bit stuffy and a public school type but he spoke fluent Arabic. He went into the field himself. His commitment bordered on activism."

But A- was on a roll. "I hold the best Queen's birthday celebrations? Isn't that right?" He looked around for approval but these were statements rather than questions. I had been to one such ambassadorial celebration in Central Asia some time ago. The host country's great and good raise a toast to Her Majesty and the wheels of international relations are oiled with beer and vodka for another year. They're a big deal in diplomatic circles.

"We had a Scottish theme. Aberdeen Angus beef and a whisky tasting last year," A- chuntered on. "Welsh cheese and lamb the year before." A- looked to us for approval.

"Hmm, very British," snorted Chester. The Great Scot didn't pick up on the irony of his own words.

The purpose of these Friday get-togethers in Jerusalem was for people to have a chance to speak frankly to each other free of the shackles of diplomatic protocol. To get things done. Maybe, just maybe something said or heard here could make all the difference. It was also a chance to socialise and be oneself.

We were introduced to McE-, a 'humanitarian adviser' for another Western government. His face was sweaty, he laughed when nothing funny was said and seemed oblivious to the fact that he was invading my personal space. "Of course most of this crowd don't *do* anything," he said with a dismissive wave of his hand. (This of course was not true as N-'s tear gassing in Bethlehem bore witness.) "They're coordinators. But nothing really ever gets done." McE- laughed again and I wondered what he himself actually did and why he was here at all if he thought that everyone's work here was pointless. He asked quite a bit about me and Chester and our plans but was rather evasive when we asked about his own career.

I wondered if McE- was a spy and that I had won the unspoken competition at these events. The game goes like this: spot the CIA, MI5 or, please God no, the Shin Bet man or woman who was not here to coordinate, conspire or advise but rather to watch us and report back on any errant leanings. Was I the lucky winner? McE- cut across my thoughts.

"I don't believe he's your son," he said unconvincingly moving far too near my face. "Fifty-five! How do you keep in such good shape?" I am easily flattered and proceeded to tell our new, laughing friend not only about my fitness regime but also full details of our plans to travel through the Palestinian Territories to Jordan. In fact it was Chester who clicked first.

"Dad, why do you always attract them?" he whispered.

"Eh?"

"That guy was hitting on you."

McE- finally left, perhaps to pump his next prey for intel. I laughed self-consciously like McE- had done but kept my own diplomatic silence and went for another beer. International diplomacy. Now is that a game or a lifestyle?

To the country that doesn't exist

April 2015

WE WERE A few minutes short of the border between Transnistria and Moldova when the stocky guy in front of us on the minibus turned round and spoke in broken English. "Have you got someone to meet you when you reach Tiraspol?" he said.

"Here we go," I whispered to Chester in Welsh. "They told us we'd be ripped off everywhere and look, it's started before we even cross the border." But Andreas was not Transnistrian, nor even Moldovan.

"I'll help you out at the checkpoint. You should be OK," he said. Helen gripped my hand, all three of us unsure how genuine this offer of friendship was.

The border crossing to Transnistria is no more than a Portakabin staffed by a couple of guys in broad hats who stamp a piece of paper for you. That's your visa. They also tell you to register at the hotel if you are staying more than twenty-four hours. "This is a big deal," counselled Andreas. "I was late getting over the border once and they charged me twenty euros for half an hour."

The miserable border guard in the big hat asked me where we were staying.

"Hotel Timoty. Tiraspol," I said.

He pointed to my passport and name. "Timothy. Timoty!" he said and laughed. I laughed too, nervously and maybe a little too loudly as I hurried back to the minibus. This was not the welcome the newspaper reports had told us to expect. No waiting for hours, no hostile questioning and certainly no bribes asked for or given. Just a bored border guard finding a laugh in my forename. It was all very normal.

"He's one of the good ones," said Andreas pointedly. "Some won't speak to you at all unless you speak Russian with them."

The Foreign and Commonwealth Office travel advice had been pretty clear: "The Transnistria region is not under Moldovan government control... You should exercise caution... The Embassy will do its best to provide consular help where needed. But in practice this will be very limited." So, my little family we're on our own.

You see the breakaway republic of Transnistria, the Pridnestrovian Moldavian Republic to give it its full title, or PMR for short, is not really a country at all. This narrow strip of land had been an autonomous republic within Ukraine until 1940. After the war it was merged with Moldova. Demands for recognition increased during the late 1980s, to no avail. Then as the Soviet Union was collapsing all around, and in something of a backlash to Moldovan nationalism, between 1990 and 1992 this mainly Russian-speaking region fought a war of independence against Moldova. It now has its own president, parliament, money and borders. But it is not a country. Despite having some 2,000 Russian soldiers based here, for 'security' reasons, not even Russia formally recognises it. It is only recognised by Abkhazia and South Ossetia, themselves countries that do not exist and who fought their own Russian-backed wars of 'independence' against Georgia in 2008.

Andreas was something of a stranger in this land too. He was a Greek Cypriot who had fallen in love with a Transnistrian girl who'd been picking fruit on his family farm outside Ayia Napa. He may have loved his wife but he hated Transnistria. "You should be safe here, but everyone, and I mean everyone, will try to take your money," he said.

Andreas is a civil engineer who is building hundreds of new homes in the Moldovan capital Chişinău but he commutes there from Tiraspol, the capital of Transnistria, every day in the cramped minibus. I asked him tentatively why he did it. "The wife, family. You know how it is." Andreas shrugged his shoulders. "I tried to set up my own business here in Tiraspol. But I was forced to quit by Sheriff." We looked blankly at each other. Did he mean the police? Was his meaning lost in translation? Andreas clocked our stares and explained.

"Sheriff is the name of the local football team. You may have heard of them. But it's not just a football team. It's big business here in Transnistria. They own all the supermarkets and gas stations. They sell all the Mercedes cars here. They have a finger in every pie."

Sheriff. It sounded like the Wild West, all top-down and threatening. We passed through the town of Bender and crossed the river Dniester. A Russian tank covered in camouflage netting was dug in on a traffic island at one end of the bridge. Guards in thick coats and fur hats, rifles lining their right hand sides walked back and forth. Others cowered in a bunker nearby. There was nothing to see through the drizzle, nothing for them to do and as yet no-one for them to fight. This must be the most boring posting in the Russian army.

The minibus rattled on and there just before Tiraspol proper was the FC Sheriff Stadium. It is large, modern and very impressive. The club was founded by Viktor Gushan and Ilya Kazmaly, former members of the KGB. The club dominates the Divizia Naţională, the top division in Moldovan football, and regularly gets into the European Champions League. The club's sponsor Sheriff Security Services has taken over most of the businesses in the PMR. Some contend it is truly run by Igor Smirnov, the first president of Transnistria, and is used as a front for money laundering. Sheriff also holds twenty-six seats in the PMR parliament. Nobody ever messes with the Sheriff.

"I tell you," said Andreas, "they made life so difficult for me. I had to close my business down before it had really started.

Permits for this and licences for that and then I had to employ whoever they told me to employ. This place is a hellhole. But my children. My girls. They're not growing up here."

How different things looked from the Hotel Timoty. The owner, Tatiana "Call me Tania" Fiodorova was smartly turned out and, like Andreas, very friendly. Business was not booming. It seemed like we were the only people staying there but Tania really wanted to make a good impression.

"The parliament building?" she repeated when I asked for directions to the only known tourist sight in Tiraspol. "Easy," Tania said pointing to the poorly photocopied map she'd given us. "Here we are on Karla Libknehta."

"He was an early German communist," said Chester knowingly, "shot alongside Rosa Luxemburg during the uprising in Berlin in 1919."

Transnistria has been described as the world's biggest open-air museum, a place where the Soviet Union never collapsed. The hammer and sickle still adorn the country's flag and currency. Coming here was our chance to see a supposedly still communist country. The real thing, and the indications so far were pretty good.

"Then turn left onto Lenin Ulitsa. Cross Karl Marx Square…" Tania continued patiently. That one needed no footnote from my personal tutor and guide. "And then into…"

"Twenty-two October Street," I announced triumphantly pointing at the crappy little map on the desk.

"Twenty-FIVE October Street," Tania corrected me with an admonitory turn of her head.

How could I have forgotten the date of the Bolshevik Revolution? Chester smirked. Bastard.

"Follow that down to the end and you will see Lenin himself," Tania said with a flurry.

The streets of Tiraspol are broad, tree-lined and set out in a grid formation. There's little traffic here for a supposed capital city. The people look healthy and are well turned out. Women in puffer coats push smart buggies, their children wrapped up against the late spring winds. There is a quiet order about the place. What cars there are drive slowly. In a very Germanic way people wait at red lights to cross the roads even when there is no traffic and we found ourselves unconsciously observing this ritual. The shops are full of consumer goods and the Sheriff supermarket was positively buzzing. It also had a currency exchange booth in the entrance where I bought my Transnistrian roubles.

Tiraspol reminded me of the set of *The Truman Show*. In that film Jim Carrey's whole life is orchestrated as part of a reality television series. He lives in a model suburb where everything is totally 'normal'. Everyone but he knows that the whole thing is a fake, a mock-up for the television audience. The spring weather gave Tiraspol a similarly unreal feel and as we walked the streets I felt as if we were part of some filmic cast. We'd been told that the economy of Transnistria was in the doldrums, the country propped up by questionable Russian money; that the people hate foreigners and the police would force a bribe from anyone they didn't like the look of. But it didn't seem that way to us.

"So much for the Stalinist throwback," said Helen. "Should we be disappointed?"

To most people the parliament building would have been another big disappointment. It's a solid white and pink Soviet construction. Big, bland, nothingy. Slightly ugly if truth be told. The front is pocked with external air-conditioning units which stick out awkwardly below every window. The real attraction though is the marble statue of Lenin which guards the small square at the front. The great man is on a great plinth, his cloak flying backwards over his left shoulder like some latter-day Winged Victory. Classical, neo-classical, socialist realist. The artistic portrayal of power doesn't change from one millennium to another. Yes, normal tourists would have been very disappointed.

"Marvellous," said Helen, "so bad that it's good."

Opposite parliament is the war memorial. Black marble

slabs list the names of the 700 men and women who died in the war of independence with Moldova. The tank mounted in front of the memorial however is Russian. "The first one to liberate Tiraspol in 1944," Tania had told us. In fact Transnistria had its very own Liberation Army which fought with honour in what the Russians call the Great Patriotic War.

The people of Transnistria are roughly thirty per cent Moldovan, thirty per cent Russian and thirty per cent Ukrainian but in a referendum in 2006, ninety-eight per cent favoured "independence and potential future integration" with Russia. It is the country's geographical position, sandwiched between Moldova and eastern Ukraine but tantalisingly close to the newly Russified Crimea, which is so problematic. The presence of the Russian troops and military hardware here keeps the Republic in a state of permanent political limbo.

After a walk along the river Dniester we sat down for lunch. I was glad Chester hadn't ordered the borscht. Below the blood-red mess of onions and potatoes lay two pieces of meat. Pork, I think. As he demolished a plate of salad and chips (a strange combination I know, but how many vegetarians are there in Transnistria?) and Helen rubbed her seemingly permanently blistered foot, the family got round to talking about perceptions of modern Russia and the geopolitical and ethnic fault lines of Europe exacerbated by mass movements of people during the time of the Soviet empire. That's what most families talk about on holiday, isn't it?

"Transnistria, South Ossetia, Abkhazia. They're all known as de facto states," pronounced Chester. "They don't really exist but they are there anyway." This college education had gone too far, but to be fair to the lad his take on things helped.

"I'm getting it now," I said. "This is not a rump communist state at all."

"Well you wouldn't get beggars in a communist state, would you?" Chester replied. We'd seen only one on the street earlier.

"And the pavements wouldn't be so higgledy-piggledy, either," ventured Helen, now awkwardly sticking a plaster onto her ankle under the table. Oh dear. My family truly believes that real communism, where there were jobs for all, the pavements were perfectly paved and the trains ran on time, actually existed.

"I suppose they just want to get on with their lives, bring up the kids and be left alone, but to do it all in Russian," I mused. The Leninabilia, hammers, sickles and communist-inspired street names were simple, historic reminders of a better past, kept alive for fear of a worse future. A crumb of comfort in a world over which you have little control. Like a human appendix, they served no real purpose bar being easy targets for sloppy Western journalists to poke fun at.

Tania was there again on reception when we returned to the Hotel Timoty with a big smile on her face. Had she been waiting for us? I was nervous about asking her directly about the politics of this country that doesn't exist but she was happy to give us her take.

"The economy is not so good here and a lot of people move away to work. My son is in Canada and works in the oil industry. Those who can leave..." she said with a small sigh, "... have already left."

"Would it help if you were part of Moldova?" I was keen not to lead or insult Tania. "Or Russia?"

"We just want to be recognised so that we can trade. There are lots of different nationalities here. We all live peacefully together," and Tania rattled off her own list of harmonious fellow Transnistrians: Moldovans, ethnic Armenians, Russians, Belarusians. A recent television report had told of discrimination against Ukrainian speakers and Moldovans simply for being Moldovan, regardless of which language they spoke. Tania hadn't heard anything like this.

"We even have Uzbeks here," she said as if this clinched the multicultural deal. Tania would take being a part of Russia if she had to but recognition by the wider world of Transnistria's sovereignty is what she really wanted.

Russia has tried to broker a deal between Moldova and

Transnistria, a fact the Western narrative overlooks. The PMR is a tiny corridor of land buffering eastern Ukraine and Moldova. The danger of the continuing political paralysis is that someone might try to break it, and that they would do so for purely political reasons. Any violation of 'Russian' rights for example, a simple border dispute or ethnic incident, could give President Putin an excuse to defend his brothers and sisters. In doing so it would open a clear path across Ukraine to Moldova. Russia seems desperate to keep Ukraine from the hands of NATO and could do the same thing here as it has done in the Donbas. The proxy war between the East and the West was again being played out in someone else's back yard and at someone else's expense.

In 1944 150,000 Red Army soldiers lost their lives crossing the River Dniester. A lot has been invested here in every sense of the word. Some people, like Viorel Ciboratu from the European Institute for Political Studies of Moldova, thinks conflict is likely. He said, "The EU needs to act fast to give Moldova a security guarantee and a clear roadmap to EU membership. This has to be a strategic decision, not economic or political."

That night we dined at the Kumanëk restaurant which was set back from the road between the river and Lenin Street. "It's traditional," we'd been told. The dry Solaricco bianco wine was clearly marked Pridnestrovie and was very good. It came from the Kvint company which also makes fantastic brandy. It's like Armenian brandy, is full of caramel and it sticks to the side of the glass, only it's a quarter of the price.

The extended family opposite us at the Kumanëk were in fine form celebrating the father's birthday. Two young girls played with toys which were spilling from a big plastic chest while the unsure thirteen year old sat at the table with the adults. A regular family enjoying a regular night out. Despite there being only us and them here for dinner we were serenaded by a piano accordion and violin playing to an electronic backing track. The music was a jumble of folk songs and jazz. Helen said the mix of the modern and traditional extended to the toilet. "I wasn't going to crouch on one of those horrid food stand things. No pan and no seat. Yuck. But then there was an amazing electronic soap dispenser and a really powerful hand dryer. It's all a bit weird."

There aren't many restaurants in Tiraspol but the next night we were again shown some marvellous hospitality. Our host Igor would look up any words he could not translate on his iPhone. He handed us a wooden pallet with five holes in it, each hole holding a glass of flavoured vodka. "Go on! Just try them and tell me what they are," Igor said. "We make them ourselves right here." Lemon was easy, so was orange. The ginger one took a bit longer and Helen was the unfortunate one who had first dibs on the garlic flavoured vodka. Igor had saved the best for last and despite his hand gestures and descriptions he had to turn to his phone when we couldn't find a word to describe it. "Horseradish," he said with a flourish. "This is my gift to you."

Wherever we had been in Tiraspol we had been warmly welcomed. I wondered aloud whether it was only visitors like us who talked about the future of Transnistria. Did the locals ponder their future each and every day? "Do they really care?" said Chester throwing a hand towards the other table in the restaurant. "Look at them. They're just getting on with it and from what I can see, they all seem to be doing OK. This is no totalitarian throwback, whatever we've been told." Chester was right of course, but I couldn't help wondering for how long they all – Tania, Andreas, the extended family at the Kumanёk, and whoever the Sheriff is – would be left alone to just get on with it.

Red Dogs, Red Dragons – from TNS to Bucharest

May 2015

IT WAS A football trip I could frankly have done without. It was 6.15 a.m. and we had just got off the overnight train from Chişinău to Bucharest. We'd had some sleep in the well-worn and overheated carriage, but not much. We were dirty, tired and hungry. Time for a pick-me-up. The guy in the café at the Gare du Nord spoke very good English and was curious about my Football Association of Wales jacket. It had been a week since we'd played Israel and I was still basking in our 3–0 victory in Haifa. He pointed at the red dragon crest on the jacket.

"Where you from?" he said as he served our coffees.

"Wales. *Ţara Galilor*?" I'd learned that much Romanian during our stay.

"Ah, yes. Wales. You know TNS?" I looked bemused. He repeated one by one the letters, "T-N-S".

"Of course we do," said Chester, amazed that a random Romanian would have heard of the Welsh Premier League let alone any of its teams.

"They are always champions," replied our new friend and then grinned. "My top team. In all my bets I include TNS, Barcelona and Bayern. They are all good. Always win and always score lots of goals. They are very good for my accumulators," he said and laughed like a drain.

"It's not good if the same team wins every year," said Chester.

I think that he meant Man United and Bayern Munich as much as little TNS.

"Mmm," said the waiter, "Every country has its problems. We have a big problem here with Roma. You know – the gypsies. Always trouble."

What a pity, I thought. He was such a nice guy. I caught Helen's eye. I could read her mind. "Plonker!" But she was also urging us not to get into an argument this early in the morning. And so we left the café, the waiter and his prejudice still stunned that the international language of football now includes the words 'Welsh,' 'Premier' and 'League' as well as the letters T, N and S.

The slow train from the capital took some two slow hours to reach Buzău but we were determined not to miss the match of the day. Second versus fourth in the Romanian League, er, Division Two. It was Gloria Buzău versus Academia Argeş from Piteşti at the Gloria Stadium. No, I'd never heard of them before either but this was a family outing. Chester had chosen the destination and I knew there was no way Helen would demur.

Kick-off for all the matches on this orthodox Good Friday was eleven o'clock. It didn't feel like a holiday in Buzău but then I'm not sure we would have known the difference. It was just gone 9 a.m. when we arrived and it was certainly bustling as we walked from the station towards the main square. The ornate French and Austro-Hungarian architecture with elaborate reliefs and finickity features ended abruptly as heavy Soviet office blocks enclosed three sides of the main square. There were noticeably more Roma here than in Bucharest. They had a distinct physiognomy and dress which marked them out from the crowd. The older women wore patterned headscarves and ankle-length, wrap-around skirts.

We stopped for breakfast at a café overlooking the market which was teeming with fruit and veg. Being Easter, every other stall was selling candles in red Perspex holders which the faithful were carrying in the direction of the main church. At the next table to us sat the mother of a Roma family. She was wearing a shocking pink outfit and had worked her hair into waist-length plaits on either side of her head. Into the bottom of the plaits, she had knotted coloured threads of red and blue. It was difficult to know what was hair and what was cotton. Was it a headdress? Had they come to church for Good Friday? I don't know but it was a very striking pose. Three generations sat at the table, enjoying a Roma day out to town I suppose. A normal family doing normal stuff.

Lying in the lap of another woman a young boy, her son or nephew, played a noisy game on his mobile phone. A middle-aged man, the father perhaps, stood in a leather jacket and flat cap smoking behind them whilst the grandfather sat and sipped from a small brandy glass. There was certainly no 'problem', no 'trouble' here as our friend in Bucharest had suggested.

It was ten o'clock in the morning. I nodded to Gramps and his brandy and said to Chester, "I don't think he'll make the game somehow."

He pointed to my breakfast pint of lager and said, "And how about you?"

The Gloria Stadium is a lovely 'square' bowl with rows of empty seats running uninterrupted all around it. Behind one goal stood the Buzău Ultras, about thirty in all. Two lads swung huge banners while their girlfriends sat dangling their legs over of the wall at the bottom of the stand. They tried to whip up some sort of atmosphere. The chants repeated 'Gloria', 'Ultras' and 'Buzău' in different combinations but with a total crowd of some 400 in an 18,000-capacity stadium they were never going to make much of an impression.

The words 'Gloria Buzău' were picked out in the main stand opposite in the club's blue-and-red colours. Chester loves Eastern European floodlights like we used to have in British football grounds and the Gloria Stadium did not disappoint. Four cumbersome *War of the Worlds*-type beasts overlooked each corner, ready to pounce on us mortals and annihilate. The whole place was open to the elements and the sun and rain had turned the red seats a rather sad washed-out pink.

The local Jandarmerie and a row of private security men heavily kitted out in riot gear moved in to guard the entrance to the tunnel as kick-off approached. They had been in charge of frisking us on the way in. I wondered whether this way over-the-top security was a throwback to communist times. In a one-party state with no freedom of association or expression any major gathering of people, and that basically meant football games, had the potential for protest and were heavily policed. I guess the thinking went, 'Well, they have the numbers, all they need is a cause.' And boy, didn't the Romanians under Ceauşescu have cause.

Yet there wasn't a hint of aggro. In fact, the security guys in their pseudo-military uniforms and body armour all left at half-time. Chester and I decided to stretch our legs and followed them. Was there one hell of a fight going on outside? It seemed unlikely as there was no sign of any Academia support in the ground. The heavies crossed the road and came back, with little plastic cups of coffee.

The game was a dour affair with poor decision making by both sets of players; wayward passes and dreadful play-acting when anyone was tackled. Chester and I tried to compare it with what we watched at home.

"Welsh Prem?" I ventured. I thought of our international ambassadors TNS.

"Well, I saw a League One game earlier this year and it was better than this," countered Chester. We settled on Conference standard.

The second half offered the same drab fayre as the previous forty-five. Academia scored with a scrappy header from a deep corner. There was more play-acting before a glorious volley from twenty-five yards sealed victory for the visitors. Most of the crowd started to leave before the final whistle and there was some abuse from the Ultras directed at the home bench. Three or four players took their chances and went over to thank the Gloria faithful. And that was that.

The next night in Bucharest was a very different affair.

OK, so it did not involve Steaua but it was a Bucharest derby. Rapid versus the Red Dogs of Dinamo. Chester had done his homework and he marched us onto an underground train and across the city to the Stadionul Dinamo. It was set in a hollow off a busy main road and was a rather pleasant place with a cluster of trees behind one side of the ground.

"It's a bit quiet here," I said. "It's only an hour to kick-off and it's a bit, well, er, quiet." There was no-one hanging around, no ticket booths or stewards or anything. I asked the lonely guy on the gate who had ignored us when we had walked past him to the wire fence at the back of the stand what was going on.

"Where's the game? Against Rapid?" I said.

"Not here," he replied. "You must go to the Arena Naţională."

Oh dear.

Dinamo's ground, we learned later, was not up to the required standard, and the game had to be played in the national stadium. We got back on the Tube and eventually found ourselves walking alongside the Dinamo fans through a pleasant suburb to the stadium. No mistake this time.

Founded in 1948, Dinamo were the sports club of the Romanian Ministry of the Interior. In the immediate aftermath of the 1989 revolution there was an attempt to abandon the name as it had become associated with Romania's secret police, the Securitate. 'Unirea Tricolor,' the name of a pre Second World War Bucharest team, was briefly adopted but it didn't catch on and so Dinamo continue to be Dinamo.

Rapid are the team of the workers and are the oldest of the Bucharest big three, having been founded in the 1920s by workers at the Grivita works in the north-west of the city. Interestingly, Gheorghe Gheorghiu-Dej, Romania's brutal communist leader who led the country from 1947 to 1965, organised a famous strike in the same rail yard in 1933 which led to his arrest and imprisonment.

It may have been a legacy of these old intra-communist rivalries but there was an even stronger police presence at the

National Arena than we had witnessed in Buzău. We were all frisked at the turnstile and Helen had her bag searched. The lady security guard took a fancy to her MAC 'Limited Edition' lipstick and confiscated it. Lipstick as a projectile eh? I have no idea of the significance of MAC or indeed the Limited Edition tag but Helen was tamping.

"Three quid for a ticket to get in and I lose a £25 lipstick. This better be good." And as a spectacle rather than for the football, it was.

When we bought our tickets at the booth outside the main stand the guy had asked us where wanted to sit.

"Where the noise is," Chester said, excitedly.

"Hmm," was the response, and he cast an eye over our little family, "with the hooligans then?" And so we joined the 2,500 or so Dinamo faithful behind the goal. In terms of the supporters it was basically us against their crowd behind the opposite goal. There were very few spectators in the stands along the sides of the pitch. Now when it is full with 55,000 Romanians the Arena Naţională must rock. But despite our best efforts the Rapid fans were penned into the opposite terrace, seemingly miles away, and the bowl felt just a bit hollow.

The game started well. An own goal gave Dinamo the lead on three minutes. Cue the first in a series of loud booms from our left hand side. A crowd of about fifty Ultras had been allowed pitchside. They were penned in by the security bods on either side and below them there was a long drop to the playing surface. But they threw firecrackers every few minutes onto the pitch with apparent impunity. We watched the telltale silver-white light fizzle against the green of the grass for a couple of seconds before a flash and then a bang ricochetted towards us. The players seemed oblivious to it all simply playing around and jumping over the wispy trails of smoke.

In the second half 'we' scored again through Bogdan Gavrila. Our fans went mad and so did the opposition. Flares were lit and poles javelined at the police in the stand opposite us. The police countered with the first of three baton charges. The crowd scattered and a handful made it to safety onto the next empty terrace. Back and forth it went but the game carried on as normal. The threats and chants from both ends all seemed a bit pointless. We were miles apart and the stands around the Rapid section were completely empty. There were no other fans to attack. It looked like a training exercise for the police.

As the game drew to a close Niculae, who'd had a superb game, was substituted and we all cheered his slow walk to the dugout. He high-fived his teammates and then jogged smartly down the touchline towards us. With an athletic leap he was up over the barrier and into the crowd below us. No official, no security man tried to stop him. Fans surged down towards him and Niculae disappeared into a sea of red shirts and scarves. As things calmed down a little he re-emerged shoulder high while one fan after another took selfies with their hero.

In this country there would have been an FA inquiry and some serious tut-tutting from Gary Lineker and the team at such rash "and potentially dangerous behaviour". Welsh Premier League it most certainly was not. But this was Romania and the bond between players and fans, on this showing at least, seemed to be still intact. What became of Helen's expensive lipstick at the Arena Națională that night however will remain a mystery.

Red Dragons

THE STORY OF WELSH FOOTBALL

Phil Stead

Lolfa

Includes the road to France

£9.99

Kicking Off in North Korea is just one of a
whole range of publications from Y Lolfa.
For a full list of books currently in print, send
now for your free copy of our new full-colour
catalogue. Or simply surf into our website

www.ylolfa.com

for secure on-line ordering.

y Lolfa

TALYBONT CEREDIGION CYMRU SY24 5HE
e-mail ylolfa@ylolfa.com
website www.ylolfa.com
phone (01970) 832 304
fax 832 782